# TEAM TRAINING ESSENTIALS

*Team Training Essentials* succinctly outlines best practices for team training, based on the latest organizational psychology research. Organized into five "pillars," this clear, accessible guide covers all aspects of team training, from design and delivery to evaluation, transfer, and sustainment methods. Useful for anyone studying team dynamics and performance as well as group training, this book will also be of interest to professionals looking to apply team training practices in real business settings.

**Eduardo Salas** is Trustee Chair and Pegasus Professor of Psychology at the University of Central Florida. He also holds an appointment as Program Director for Human Systems Integration Research Department at the Institute for Simulation and Training.

# TEAM TRAINING ESSENTIALS

## A Research-Based Guide

*Eduardo Salas*
*with*
*Lauren Benishek*
*Chris Coultas*
*Aaron Dietz*
*Rebecca Grossman*
*Elizabeth Lazzara*
*James Oglesby*

Routledge
Taylor & Francis Group

NEW YORK AND LONDON

First published 2015
by Routledge
711 Third Avenue, New York, NY 10017

and by Routledge
27 Church Road, Hove, East Sussex BN3 2FA

*Routledge is an imprint of the Taylor & Francis Group, an informa business*

*Library of Congress Cataloging-in-Publication Data*

Library of Congress Control Number: 2014958677

ISBN: 978-1-138-81421-9 (hbk)
ISBN: 978-1-138-81422-6 (pbk)
ISBN: 978-1-315-74764-4 (ebk)

Typeset in Bembo
by Apex CoVantage, LLC

Printed and bound in the United States of America by Publishers Graphics,
LLC on sustainably sourced paper.

# CONTENTS

*Foreword*　　　　　　　　　　　　　　　　　　*vii*
*Preface*　　　　　　　　　　　　　　　　　　　*ix*
*Acknowledgments*　　　　　　　　　　　　　　*xi*

1　Introduction　　　　　　　　　　　　　　　1
　　*Teams, Teamwork, and Team Performance 2*
　　*Team Training 6*
　　*Book Overview 8*
　　*The Pillars of Team Training 10*

2　Pillar 1: Ensure the Need for Teamwork Behaviors
　　and Team Training　　　　　　　　　　　　18
　　*Principle 1: Systematically Identify Characteristics*
　　　*of the Organization, Team Tasks, and Individual*
　　　*Team Members 19*
　　*Principle 2: Evaluate Whether the Organization*
　　　*Is Ready to Receive Team Training 25*

3　Pillar 2: Create a Positive Team Training Climate
　　for Learning and the Learner　　　　　　　31
　　*Principle 3: Generate Support from Organizational*
　　　*Leadership 33*
　　*Principle 4: Prepare and Motivate the Learner*
　　　*for Team Training 36*
　　*Principle 5: Provide a Safe, Non-Critical Team*
　　　*Training Environment 43*

4   Pillar 3: Design Team Training for Maximum Accessibility,
    Usability, and Learnability                                        52
    *Principle 6: Systematically Design Team Training Based*
        *on What's Scientifically Shown to Be Effective  53*
    *Principle 7: Leverage Information Presentation,*
        *Demonstration, Practice, and Feedback  63*
    *Principle 8: Employ Team Training Delivery Strategies,*
        *Tools, and Technology Appropriate for Meeting*
        *the Needs of the Organization, Team, and Trainees  70*
    *Principle 9: Ensure Instructors Are Prepared to Teach  76*

5   Pillar 4: Evaluate the Team Training Program                       85
    *Principle 10: Determine What to Measure During*
        *Team Training and How You Will Measure It  86*
    *Principle 11: Analyze If the Team Training Program*
        *Was Successful and Determine Why It Was Effective*
        *(or Not)  94*

6   Pillar 5: Create a System for Enduring and Sustaining
    Teamwork Behaviors in Organizations                              103
    *Principle 12: Establish Mechanisms for the Continued*
        *Assessment and Improvement of Team Training  104*
    *Principle 13: Provide Opportunities to Foster*
        *Continual Team Improvement  107*
    *Principle 14: Motivate and Facilitate the Long-Term*
        *Transfer and Sustainment of Teamwork Behaviors  111*

7   Concluding Remarks                                                123
    *The Science of Team Training  124*
    *What Team Training Is NOT  125*

*Appendix 1*                                                          131
*Appendix 2*                                                          151
*Appendix 3*                                                          157
*Appendix 4*                                                          161
*Appendix 5*                                                          163
*Index*                                                               169

# FOREWORD

The NASA Human Research Program has the job of mitigating the major risks to human health and performance in long-duration space flight. We do this with the eventual goal of sending humans to Mars. During such a mission, the crew will be very much on its own, as real-time communication with mission control will be impossible due the transit time of radio communications over such large distances (15 minutes or more, each way). Crews will also, despite the best efforts of mission planners and life-science researchers, have to confront a variety of issues that have not been specifically considered or accounted for. Both of these factors mean that any crew that goes to Mars (or on any similarly challenging journey) must work as a tightly integrated and high-performing team. While the usual lengthy and intense preflight training regimen for spaceflight crews provides many opportunities for team building, a focused and efficient approach that makes use of the newest findings in team-training research would benefit all parties involved. That is where the material presented in this book can be of great use.

—*Mark J. Shelhamer, NASA,*
*Human Research Program, USA*

# PREFACE

Teamwork matters in our lives today more than ever. It matters in aviation, the military, and in the oil and nuclear power industries. It matters in the corporate world, in sports teams, healthcare, and in multidisciplinary scientific collaborations. Teamwork matters not only because it drives organizational productivity, innovation, and overall well-being, but because many times, people's lives depend on effective teamwork. Yet teamwork does not come naturally. It is rare, hard, elusive, multidimensional, and episodic. Accordingly, team members must develop the knowledge, skills, and attitudes that contribute to effective teamwork. This is where team training has a critical role.

This book was written with the motivation of providing simple and practical, yet simultaneously elegant and prescriptive guidance on how to design, deliver, implement, evaluate, and ensure the transfer of team training. It is not a handbook or a review of the topic. It is an effort to translate a large body of knowledge—what we know about good learning and training design, what we know about team effectiveness and teamwork—into practical guidance. It is intended for team training designers, instructors, and practitioners who have been searching for explicit guidance, suggestions, tips, or a resource to start, adapt, or modify a context-specific team training program. While the information presented within this book exists in the literature in many forms, and it has been placed in myriad sources with varying degrees of empirical support, much of the guidance is mostly inaccessible or piecemeal. We try here to integrate these bodies of knowledge. While the focus of this work is team training, much of this guidance relates to training in general, making this a worthwhile resource for a wider audience.

This book has been largely the effort of the doctoral students (noted as co-collaborators) in the Industrial and Organizational Psychology, and the Applied

Experimental and Human Factors Psychology programs at the University of Central Florida, under my guidance. They deserve much of the credit for what is done herein. To all of them, my gratitude.

We hope this book helps those in positions where teamwork is paramount to safety, security, space exploration, quality, productivity, job satisfaction, and employee well-being. We hope it provides some practical insights, prescriptions, and an evidence-based roadmap for the design, delivery, evaluation, and transfer of team training.

*Eduardo Salas*
*University of Central Florida*

# ACKNOWLEDGMENTS

This work was supported by a grant from the National Aeronautics and Space Administration (#NNX09AK48G). Any opinions, findings, and conclusions or recommendations expressed in this material are those of the authors and do not necessarily reflect the views of NASA. We would like to thank Lauren Leveton, Laura Bollweg from NASA, and Brandon Vessey from EASI/Wyle for their support and encouragement through the grant and this project. This work builds on a previous unpublished manuscript authored by Eduardo Salas, Katherine Wilson, Christin Upshaw, and Deborah DiazGranados. We would like to thank Shawn Burke (University of Central Florida, Institute for Simulation and Training), Bill O'Keefe (NASA/United Space Alliance), and Synnove Nesse (Falck Nutec, Norway) for their feedback on previous drafts of this document.

# 1

# INTRODUCTION

Teams are a way of life in organizations. They afford organizations a competitive advantage by providing complex, innovative, and comprehensive solutions to organizational challenges (Gladstein, 1984; Hackman, 1987; Moreland & Levine, 1992; Sundstrom, DeMeuse, & Futrell, 1990). This advantage occurs because as a work structure, teams offer an opportunity to merge diverse perspectives and skills to improve the overall quality of the team's outcomes. Further, teams have the potential to adapt to changing environments by providing a means to distribute work functions to reduce work overload and to identify errors and alternative strategies when necessary. Despite the great potential teams hold for improving the effectiveness of organizations and performing tasks that are not able to be accomplished by an individual alone, many teams fail and this can have severe consequences (e.g., loss of profit, loss of life). Additionally, if asked, many employees acknowledge that working in teams is more complex because of the increased difficulty in achieving consensus on a plan of action, frequent miscommunication or lack of communication, and the tension felt in asking individuals with different work habits, capabilities, and constraints to conform to the "team's way" of getting work done. As a result, organizations and their employees have a love-hate relationship with teams.

Teams may unfairly receive this reputation due to negative experiences (e.g., excessive or needless conflict, social loafing) that may occur while working with others. This may be caused by the laissez-faire assumption common among organizations that teams "just happen," that employees will naturally understand how to manage the complex dynamics inherent to team functioning (e.g., conflicting personalities, work preferences, competing work commitments). Consequently, teams and team members frequently do not have the requisite skills for effective teamwork, leading many employees to see teams as something they must endure, rather than a method to achieve more than the sum of their individual inputs. The fact of the matter is that teams do not "just happen." Teams require training to facilitate more effective team processes (Hackman, 1998). Until the science of team training (Salas & Cannon-Bowers, 2001) is more widely used in our organizations, teams will likely continue to underachieve.

Given the importance of—and difficulties associated with—teams and teamwork, the purpose of this book is to provide research-based guidance for the effective design, delivery, transfer (i.e., training that leads to improvements on the job), and maintenance (i.e., training that leads to long-term improvements) of team training. Chapter 1 provides the reader with a brief overview of teams, teamwork, and team training to provide structure for the content that is presented throughout this book. We also outline the remaining chapters, which are delineated into five pillars of team training. Briefly, these pillars address essential concepts for effective team training; we present them as easily digestible, action-oriented statements: (1) *Ensure the Need for Teamwork Behaviors and Team Training*, (2) *Create a Positive Climate for Learning and the Learner*, (3) *Design Team Training for Maximum Accessibility, Learnability, and Usability*, (4) *Evaluate the Team Training Program*, and (5) *Create a System for Enduring and Sustaining Teamwork Behaviors in Organizations*. These pillars are described in greater detail later in this chapter and fully explicated in their respective chapters. It is our hope that this book will provide a clear and practical way in which team training can be developed, implemented, evaluated, and sustained for any type of team.

## Teams, Teamwork, and Team Performance

In the modern working world, teams have become a mainstay of organizational life. Retail stores have different sales teams in different departments responsible for selling products and assisting customers, while management teams lead these teams and make operational decisions. Research and development teams consist of multiple researchers who collectively innovate and improve products. Teams of military personnel work together in dangerous, high-risk, and time-sensitive environments to protect national security. First responder teams collaborate in similar environments to rescue civilians, protect property, and provide order. It seems as if no work of consequence is accomplished completely independent of others. No matter the setting, the axiom that "no man is an island," seems to be truer now than ever.

Why this reliance on teams, though? In part, this is due to the increasing complexity and competition present within the current organizational landscape (Allen & Hecht, 2004; Bush & Hattery, 1956; Wuchty, Jones, & Uzzi, 2007). Increasing complexity means that it is becoming even rarer that one individual can be completely responsible for the production, development, or provision of any particular good, product, or service. Even a job that might typically be considered a one-person operation—that of a novelist—is in actuality reliant on teams, as the novelist will require a team of agents, editors, and publishers to fully develop, promote, and distribute the book. Furthermore, as technological developments continue to level the playing field amongst economic competitors, organizations must search for new sources of competitive advantage. Teams are often considered to be one source of competitive advantage, as it is often thought that teams promise synthesis and exponential possibilities. In other words, teams may be advantageous because (when functioning correctly) they can produce more than the sum of their component members operating independently (Stagl, Burke, Salas, & Pierce, 2006).

## Defining Teams and Teamwork

In an effort to implement teams in organizations, the term "team" has been hastily applied to departments, divisions, and groups of individuals without first considering what actually defines a team. The distinction between a team versus a group is an ongoing debate in the research community (Guzzo & Dickson, 1996; Moreland, Argote, & Krishnan, 2002; Saavendra, Earley, & Van Dyne, 1993; Tannenbaum, Beard, & Salas, 1992). For the purposes of this book, however, we define a team as *two or more people whose tasks are in some way interdependent (i.e., individual efforts are dependent upon the efforts of other members) and who have shared, common goals* (Dyer, 1984; Kozlowski & Bell, 2003; Salas, Dickenson, Converse, & Tannenbaum, 1992).

A common framework for conceptualizing team performance is to depict teams as having inputs, mediators (i.e., processes or emergent states), and outcomes (Kozlowski & Ilgen, 2006; LePine, Piccolo, Jackson, Mathieu, & Saul, 2008). Inputs are those things that feed into the team performance dynamic. These consist of variables characteristic of: (1) the component team members (e.g., skills and attitudes, personality, cognitive ability), (2) the team overall (e.g., team size, structure, task), and (3) the overall organization (e.g., higher leadership, climate, organizational size). Outcomes, naturally, refer to the results of team interaction—ranging from relatively objective metrics of team performance (e.g., sales, efficiency, safety) to more subjective indices (e.g., team and individual job satisfaction). As shown in Figure 1.1, team inputs do not directly translate into effective team performance outcomes. Instead, the effects of team inputs on outcomes are mediated—or transmitted—through teamwork processes and emergent states.

Team processes are defined as *"members' interdependent acts that convert inputs to outcomes through cognitive, verbal, and behavioral activities directed toward organizing taskwork to achieve collective goals"* (Marks, Mathieu, & Zaccaro, 2001, p. 357). Team processes can be further categorized as action processes (i.e., those involved when executing a task), transition processes (i.e., those involved when planning, preparing, or reflecting on a task), or interpersonal processes (LePine et al., 2008; Marks et al., 2001). Action processes include such team behaviors as

**FIGURE 1.1.** Overview of IMO Framework.

communicating between members, monitoring effective performance, and assisting teammates when they need help on specific task components (i.e., "backup behaviors"). Transition processes primarily (but not only) occur when teams interact but are not engaged in directly performing the primary task; these processes can consist of providing feedback, generating a vision for future task performance cycles, or reassigning roles to different members. Interpersonal processes occur during both action and transition phases of the team performance cycle, and include things such as conflict management and resolution, developing norms for social interaction, and monitoring/managing the emotional atmosphere (e.g., through encouragement behaviors).

Where team processes simply refer to different types of collective behavior, emergent states (while still a mediating variable between inputs and outcomes) are somewhat more esoteric. Generally, they refer to cognitive and affective variables that are held by individual team members but also exist at the team level and influence team outcomes. Cognitive emergent states include things that influence the ways in which teams collect, interpret, process, and store information, such as transactive memory systems (i.e., the state of team members' knowledge of what other team members know) and shared mental models (i.e., the collective understanding or mental representation of how different team- or task-relevant variables are interrelated). Affective emergent states, on the other hand, refer to the collective attitudes and feelings within the group such as interpersonal trust, cohesion (i.e., the bond felt toward the task and/or the team), and psychological safety (i.e., the sense that taking interpersonal risks will not be met with negative reactions). Emergent states are partly aggregate manifestations of individual experiences, but as these variables emerge, they come to describe the team itself to a certain extent. For this reason, emergent states are sometimes considered to be both a mediating variable and an outcome of team inputs and processes (Marks et al., 2001).

## Teamwork and Taskwork

Ultimately, team processes and emergent states transmit (or mediate) the effects of team inputs on outcomes. Broadly speaking, team processes and emergent states are closely linked to two things that are necessary for accomplishing shared and interdependent tasks—taskwork and teamwork. Taskwork refers to those relevant behaviors that directly lead to the successful accomplishment of collective goals; furthermore, these behaviors are generally actions that individual team members execute and do not directly rely on other team members' input. Teamwork consists of the interdependent interactions among team members as they work towards completing their objectives—including the interpersonal behaviors that facilitate effective and harmonious interactions between team members. Teamwork behaviors include (among other things) coordinating actions between members, adapting to the changing environment, and anticipating each other's needs to reach the overarching team goals (Kozlowski & Bell, 2003).

> **Taskwork:** Working on a specific duty of one's job.
> **Teamwork:** Coordination, cooperation, and communication among individuals to achieve a shared goal.

The distinction between taskwork and teamwork is important, because teams that are equipped with appropriate taskwork skills (e.g., manipulating flight controls) may not be similarly equipped with the accompanying teamwork skills (e.g., communication between flight crew and cabin crew members) essential for effective team performance. Given the importance of both of these domains to team performance, those interested in the success and development of teams—trainers, leaders, and team members themselves—must be cognizant not only of generic performance metrics, but of the specific task and team processes underlying team performance. And while team training can indeed teach the team to perform taskwork skills, these skills are often highly context specific and are therefore outside the scope of this work. Teamwork skills, on the other hand, are generalizable to a wide variety of situations and are frequently the focus of team training interventions. Accordingly, we briefly review them here.

**Teamwork skills and competencies.** Teamwork skills and competencies are broad components of effective teamwork that are multifaceted, complex, and often difficult to measure (Rosen, Salas, Silvestri, Wu, & Lazzara, 2008). Indeed, the domain of team competencies is vast and complex. While the broad factors that influence teamwork were introduced in Figure 1.1, some of these factors (e.g., context, composition, culture) are not internal to the team's functioning and as such are not influenced by team training (though they absolutely influence team training effectiveness). Kraiger, Ford, and Salas (1993) proposed a heuristic for evaluating training that is also relevant for discussing the teamwork skills and competencies often focused on as a part of team training. This heuristic consists of the attitudes, behaviors, and cognitions (i.e., the "ABCs") that change within an individual (or in our case, a team) as a result of training. The "ABCs" heuristic is helpful in classifying the attitudes, behaviors, and cognitions that drive team effectiveness as well. Some of these factors are illustrated in Figure 1.2, though a more complete description (including definitions of the

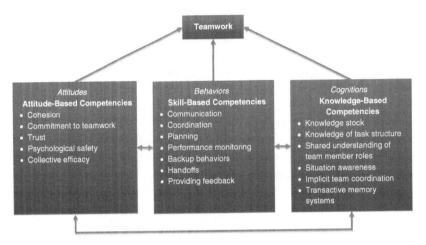

**FIGURE 1.2.** The *A*ttitudes, *B*ehaviors, and *C*ognitions (ABCs) That Influence Teamwork. Adapted from: Salas & Cannon-Bowers, 2000, p. 315.

various teamwork constructs) can be seen in Appendix 1 (Salas, Rosen, Burke, & Goodwin, 2009).

## Team Training

Most organizations do not assume that their employees come equipped with all of the necessary *taskwork* competencies, and accordingly offer training to gain skills essential for successful task performance (e.g., technical procedures, Microsoft package tutorials, presentation skills training, etc.). What these organizations neglect, however, is the need to provide employees with training on *teamwork* competencies. Indeed, training for teamwork becomes more important as teams themselves become more complex. Greater complexity means that it becomes increasingly difficult to extract maximum benefit out of team-based structures. Part of this complexity can be attributed to the growing prevalence of globalization and distributed teams. As the world shrinks, cross-cultural interactions are more frequent, and multicultural teams become more common. Cultural gaffes and misunderstandings can make multicultural teams difficult to manage or work in. Additionally, distributed teams—teams that work together toward a shared goal, but are not in the same physical location or at the same time—can be quite effective, but this separation makes teamwork more difficult. Interventions to improve team functioning have therefore become critically important to today's organizations.

Unfortunately, when organizations recognize that teamwork is lacking, the initial response is often team-building activities such as ropes courses, icebreakers, and other "getting to know your teammate" activities. These team-building interventions seem to be beneficial for clarifying and defining team roles (Shuffler, Burke, Kramer, & Salas, 2012), but beyond this, research on their effectiveness has been inconsistent, making it unclear whether or not they even have meaningful benefits (Buller, 1986; Salas, Rozell, Mullen, & Driskell, 1999; Sundstrom et al., 1990; Tannenbaum et al., 1992; Woodman & Sherwood, 1980).

Unlike team building, team training strategies have been proven successful at improving teamwork in organizations and are just as important as taskwork training (Salas et al., 2008). Team training differs from team building interventions in that team training follows the same science-based guidelines as any other kind of taskwork training. That is, organizations must first understand the competencies needed for effective team processes and develop training around the identified competencies. After implementing the training, the organization must evaluate the effectiveness of the team training program as to whether team members are able to demonstrate the desired knowledge, skills, and attitudes (KSAs) and transfer the KSAs to the workplace.

Salas and Cannon-Bowers (2000) define team training as a set of tools and methods used to train a group of individuals on both task-related individual competencies and teamwork competencies. This process should yield unbiased assessments of performance and provide behavior-based feedback. They go on to explain that "team training is not simply a location where a set of individuals go to engage in task-relevant exercises; it is not necessarily a single program; it is not a simulation per se; nor is it necessarily a network of interconnected individuals" (p. 313). Instead, team training involves scientifically grounded development and delivery of training content and instructional strategies, systematic evaluation, and mechanisms to ensure the successful transfer of trained skills to the work context and the sustainment of those skills over time. The chapters throughout this book will present research-based guidance relevant to all phases of the team training cycle, including before, during, and after team training.

In general, team training is provided to instill KSAs (e.g., conflict management and resolution, communication, coordination and organization) that will improve job performance, team performance, and organizational effectiveness. In the past, training focused on the individual, because it was assumed that learning occurred at the individual level. While this is true to an extent, due to global changes in how work is done (e.g., faster, cheaper) and where the work occurs (e.g., flexible work schedules, distributed teams), organizations must provide employees with continuous learning opportunities that are not only just in time, but focused on the "soft skills" (e.g., interpersonal skills, conflict resolution, assertiveness) essential for collaboration in the changing environment. Thus, team training not only trains at the individual level but also provides opportunities for team members to learn and interact together so as to simulate the conditions under which the trained KSAs will be used.

Team training can be a powerful solution for improving organizational outcomes and safety. Salas and colleagues (2008) conducted a meta-analytic investigation to evaluate the overall effectiveness of team training reported in 45 studies representing 2,650 teams. Their results demonstrate support (about 20%

performance improvement) for team training as a mechanism for improving team-level cognitive outcomes (i.e., knowledge), affective outcomes (i.e., beliefs and attitudes), behavioral processes (e.g., communication), and performance. While team training clearly has potential as a mechanism for improving team processes and outcomes, careful consideration must be given to determining what and whom to train, how best to implement team training, how to gauge team training effectiveness, and how to promote the transfer and maintenance of trained KSAs. These decisions should be informed by team training science. Therefore, we designed this book as a practical reference of research-based guidance for optimal team training delivery. In the remainder of this chapter, we outline the content of this book.

## Book Overview

### *Development*

From over 25 years of research and hundreds of articles on teamwork, training, and team training, we extracted over 1,000 unique findings for effective team training. This extensive array of best practices was culled and iteratively synthesized to begin to identify thematic content areas where literature findings converged. In so doing, we sought to reduce, summarize, and refine this large set of findings into a document that was comprehensive, yet digestible and practical. This involved countless consensus building meetings among the authors, and soliciting feedback from academic, industry, and government professionals on numerous drafts.

As we summarized the findings with an eye towards generating easily digestible takeaways, we ensured that the concepts propagated were: (1) practical, (2) backed by empirical evidence and scholarly support, (3) sufficiently meaningful as standalone statements, and (4) unique from other concepts discussed in this work. This process yielded an easily accessible, hierarchical, and practical organizational structure. Each chapter starts at a very high level and becomes increasingly fine-grained, enabling the reader to more intuitively digest guidance for how to best design, implement, evaluate, and sustain team training. The structure is made up of: (1) broad **pillars**, which encompass (2) more specific **principles** of team training, which frame even more specific (3) **guidelines** for team training, which are comprised of (4) the specific **tips and advice** that were extracted from our comprehensive literature review. In the section below, we briefly define each of these structural terms. Before further clarifying the structure and content of this book, however, a brief caveat is appropriate.

The training literature is extremely broad but is spearheaded by several thought leaders in the field (e.g., Kevin Ford, Irwin Goldstein, Kurt Kraiger, Donald Kirkpatrick, Steve Kozlowski, John Mathieu, Raymond Noe, Scott Tannenbaum, Ken Brown, Paul Thayer, Brad Bell) who have contributed a great deal to our understanding of what makes for effective training. We have attempted to cite these and others as frequently as possible. This notwithstanding, a substantial amount of the extant literature on team performance and team training effectiveness comes from research conducted by Eduardo Salas and other researchers affiliated with not only the University of Central Florida, the Department of Psychology and the Institute for Simulation and Training (e.g., Clint Bowers, Kim Smith-Jentsch, Florian Jentsch, Steve Fiore, Shawn Burke), but also the Naval Air Warfare Center Training Systems Division (e.g., Jan Cannon-Bowers, Joan Johnston, Carol Paris, David Barber, Catherine Gonos, Renee Stout, Randy Oser, Carolyn Prince, Maureen Bergondy, Dan Dwyer, Katie Ricci, Gwen Campbell, Beth Blickensderfer, Melissa Walwanis) and industry and academic partners (e.g., Scott Tannenbaum, Daniel Serfaty, Marion Cohen, Steve Kozlowski, Jim Driskell, Elliot Entin, Wayne Zachary) as well. We clarify this here simply to explain that while our references may appear self-serving, this is merely a function of the volume of research currently available generated by most of those noted above.

## Structural Approach

**Tips and advice** are highly specified statements of how team training should be designed, delivered, and generally conducted (Blickensderfer, Cannon-Bowers, & Salas, 1997; Swezey & Salas, 1992). Our tips and advice have been extracted from the training and learning literature bases, as well as practical experiences (from the authors) garnered from years of conducting and researching teams and team training. These explicit statements describe very specific findings that summarize "what works" in team training.

**Guidelines** are slightly broader, though still relatively specific and prescriptive, statements that take general concepts and principles and translate them into actionable statements (Blickensderfer et al., 1997; Swezey & Salas, 1992). Guidelines are derived from unique tips and advice that converge in a general pattern to provide a somewhat broad, albeit actionable step. For example, three tips might be:

> "Shorten the delay between performance and feedback."
> "Deliver constructive, not personally critical feedback."
> "Support feedback with objective indicators of performance."

Across these three tips, the clear, general trend is to "provide informative, task-relevant feedback to trainees." The guideline is loosely prescriptive, while the tips and advice clarify and specify the guideline.

**Principles** are even broader than guidelines, and at this high level, they begin to lose some of their prescriptive ability. Principles describe what *should* happen in team training, and *why* something is necessary, but are not clear on how this normative outcome is to be accomplished. When digesting a principle, the reader is likely to agree that the concept is important, but is unclear on how to move forward (note: guidelines and tips answer the question of how). In our organizing structure, principles help frame and contextualize guidelines by explicating the outcome of several guidelines. Returning to the previous feedback example, research has revealed that feedback is important not only to encourage learning during team training, but also to enable continuous learning opportunities after the training has officially ended. So the guideline of "provide feedback" may be further understood within the context of its purpose/principle—Is the guideline intended to facilitate learning during training, or is it meant to foster continuous development post-training? Furthermore, this means that similar guidelines may appear in multiple places, if the purpose (i.e., principle) is different.

Broader still than principles are **pillars** of team training. We conceptualize pillars as the fundamental, scientifically derived, basic elements of team training. They are broad concepts that research has consistently found to be necessary for an effective team training experience. The pillars of team training, consistent with current frameworks of training design (Molenda, Reigeluth, & Nelson, 2003), emerge as the highest-order constructs spanning their respective principles, guidelines, and tips. These pillars represent the five unifying themes covering thousands of empirical findings on training and team training. Finally, it should be noted that while the pillars may be somewhat iterative or recursive, they are presented in a general chronological order. That is, Pillar 1 must be addressed before moving on to Pillar 2, Pillar 2 before Pillar 3, and so on. We briefly review these pillars here.

## The Pillars of Team Training

> Team training is a systematic, iterative, and recursive process.

The five pillars of team training are: (1) Ensure the Need for Teamwork Behaviors and Team Training, (2) Create a Positive Team Training Climate for Learning and the Learner, (3) Design Team Training for Maximum Accessibility, Usability, and Learnability, (4) Evaluate the Team Training Program, and (5) Create a System for Enduring and Sustaining Teamwork Behaviors in Organizations. Figure 1.2 illustrates a heuristic for conceptualizing the relationship among each pillar. As demonstrated throughout this book, team training is a systematic, iterative, and recursive process. Before team training can be implemented, research suggests the first question to answer is whether or not team training is even needed—this is the essence of **Pillar 1**. If there is not a need for improved teamwork, or the training is not likely to elicit the organization's desired results, then team training should not be implemented. There are two broad principles for ensuring the necessity of teamwork behaviors: (1) collecting data and (2) interpreting these data to determine whether or not to proceed with team training. In Pillar 1, various data collection strategies at the organization, team, and person levels are presented. After these data are collected, they must be interpreted to assess whether there is a need for teamwork training, and whether the training is likely to be successful or not.

Another essential component of effective team training is the creation of a training climate—that is, a commonly perceived social atmosphere defined by its values and common practices—that facilitates positive outcomes in the immediate training setting. Without a climate that supports the team training intervention, individuals will be less willing to actively engage in the training, or they may even refuse training altogether. **Pillar 2** spans three principles that, if executed correctly, will circumvent these issues, creating an enthusiastic learning climate and facilitating the training process. These principles entail obtaining support from organizational leadership, directly motivating the individuals who will be trained, and ensuring that the immediate training environment is motivating, engaging, and non-threatening.

Of course, one pillar of team training should detail how to design and implement the intervention itself. In **Pillar 3,** we describe four principles of good team training design. As it relates to design and delivery, team training should be developed systematically, not haphazardly, or with a one-size-fits-all mentality. Additionally, team training should include four hallmark features: *information presentation, demonstration, practice,* and *feedback.* Team training must also be presented (delivered) to learners (i.e., trainees), and this is typically done by an instructor, in conjunction with some kind of delivery medium or technology (e.g., booklets, simulations). These presentational principles of effective team training design and implementation discuss the need to *prepare* the instructors for training, as well as the need to select a delivery medium that is well matched to team training goals and objectives.

The effectiveness of team training (i.e., the extent to which team training goals and objectives are being realized) should be systematically considered and assessed before, during, and after team training using robust evaluation metrics that have been developed prior to team training implementation. **Pillar 4** contains two principles that focus on the importance of good measurement and evaluation strategies. First, it is necessary to determine what to measure and how it will be measured; second, measurement data should be collated and analyzed using appropriate methods to determine exactly what effects team training is having on individual team members, the team (or teams), and the organization.

Finally, it is essential that a system is in place to foster the maintenance and sustainment of the trained teamwork behaviors. If **Pillar 5** is overlooked, the initial progress that is made as a result of team training is at risk of being lost. To mitigate this threat, a system must be in place (or implemented if not already in place) that continually emphasizes and reinforces the importance of trained teamwork behaviors. The three principles of an effective training sustainment system are: (1) ongoing assessment and improvement of team training, (2) continual opportunities for relearning and practice of trained teamwork behaviors, and (3) organizational policies and practices that motivate and facilitate the continued enactment of teamwork behaviors.

Clearly, team training is a complex, systematic, recursive, and iterative endeavor. Many of these pillars transcend traditional conceptualizations that parse out team training guidance into before, during, and after training divisions (see Figure 1.3). For example, metrics to evaluate team training should be developed before team training is implemented (Pillar 4). The pillars, principles, and guidelines presented in this book are summarized in Table 1.1. The remaining chapters will provide greater detail on each of these topics.

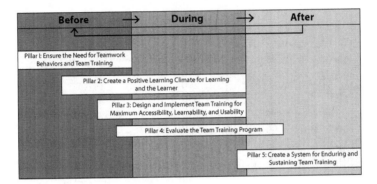

**FIGURE 1.3.** An Overview of the Pillars of Team Training.
Adapted from: Gregory, Feitosa, Driskell, & Salas, 2013.

**TABLE 1.1** Overview of Pillars, Principles, and Guidelines for Team Training

| Pillars | Principles | Guidelines |
|---------|-----------|------------|
| Pillar 1: Ensure the Need for Teamwork Behaviors and Team Training | Principle 1: Systematically identify characteristics of the organization, team tasks, and individual team members | • Guideline 1. Determine how organizational factors (e.g., culture, climate, strategic goals) may facilitate or hinder teamwork<br>• Guideline 2. Define the team's purpose and what teamwork competencies (i.e., knowledge, skills, and attitudes [KSAs]) are required to achieve team goals<br>• Guideline 3. Understand the individual characteristics likely to impact teamwork and team training |
| | Principle 2: Evaluate whether the organization is ready to receive team training | • Guideline 4. Analyze the cause of performance deficiencies and consider appropriate improvement strategies<br>• Guideline 5. Determine whether the organization can adequately support team training |

| Pillars | Principles | Guidelines |
| --- | --- | --- |
| Pillar 2: Create a Positive Team Training Climate for Learning and the Learner | Principle 3: Generate support from organizational leadership | • Guideline 6. Champion the importance of team training to leadership<br>• Guideline 7. Encourage leadership to establish systems for reinforcing and modeling desired teamwork behaviors before and during team training |
| | Principle 4: Prepare and motivate the learner for team training | • Guideline 8. Frame team training in a positive light<br>• Guideline 9. Encourage trainees to set goals prior to participating in team training<br>• Guideline 10. Encourage trainees to be engaged during team training<br>• Guideline 11. Facilitate individuals' and teams' efficacy beliefs that they will be able to successfully complete team training |
| | Principle 5: Provide a safe, non-critical team training environment | • Guideline 12. Articulate what is expected and appropriate behavior during team training<br>• Guideline 13. Frame errors positively during team training<br>• Guideline 14. Reduce any ambiguity surrounding team training |
| Pillar 3: Design Team Training for Maximum Accessibility, Usability, and Learnability | Principle 6: Systematically design team training based on what's scientifically shown to be effective | • Guideline 15. Form partnerships between subject matter experts and learning experts<br>• Guideline 16. Define learning objectives to be targeted during team training in advance<br>• Guideline 17. Select the specific teamwork knowledge, skills, and/or attitudes to be targeted in team training<br>• Guideline 18. Organize team training material in a manner that will facilitate learning<br>• Guideline 19. Select instructional strategies that foster the development of teamwork competencies<br>• Guideline 20. Pilot test team training prior to implementation |
| | Principle 7: Leverage information presentation, demonstration, practice, and feedback | • Guideline 21. Present information to trainees about the teamwork KSAs targeted in team training and why they are important<br>• Guideline 22. Demonstrate each teamwork KSA<br>• Guideline 23. Provide trainees with the opportunity to practice teamwork KSAs<br>• Guideline 24. Provide feedback to trainees on their practice performance |

(*Continued*)

**TABLE 1.1** (Continued)

| Pillars | Principles | Guidelines |
|---------|-----------|-----------|
| | Principle 8: Employ team training delivery strategies, tools, and technology appropriate for meeting the needs of the organization, team, and trainees | • Guideline 25. Use design and delivery methods that are engaging and motivating<br>• Guideline 26. Match the characteristics of the learning environment to those of the transfer environment<br>• Guideline 27. Make sure trainees are capable of using team training technology<br>• Guideline 28. Consider short- and long-term costs of team training technology<br>• Guideline 29. Establish the organizational infrastructure needed to support team training technology |
| | Principle 9: Ensure instructors are prepared to teach | • Guideline 30. Create materials to aid instructors during team training<br>• Guideline 31. Train instructors |
| Pillar 4: Evaluate the Team Training Program | Principle 10: Determine what to measure during team training and how you will measure it | • Guideline 32. Select measures that target learning objectives, core competencies and KSAs, diagnose performance, and inform meaningful and constructive feedback<br>• Guideline 33. Develop benchmarks of learning and performance to assess teamwork skills at many points throughout team training—including before team training<br>• Guideline 34. Adopt measures that capture both teamwork outcomes (e.g., mission completion, products) and teamwork processes (e.g., communication)<br>• Guideline 35. Utilize several measurement sources, techniques, and tools to capture multiple aspects of performance (e.g., individual and team performance)<br>• Guideline 36. Develop measurement tools to assess training using multiple criteria<br>• Guideline 37. Equip assessors to use measurement tools correctly |
| | Principle 11: Analyze if the team training program was successful and determine why it was effective (or not) | • Guideline 38. Establish the characteristics (i.e., reliability and validity) of the measurement tools by utilizing established research and statistical methods<br>• Guideline 39. Account for short- and long-term performance trends<br>• Guideline 40. Document and disseminate evaluation findings |

| Pillars | Principles | Guidelines |
|---|---|---|
| Pillar 5: Create a System for Enduring and Sustaining Teamwork Behaviors in Organizations | Principle 12: Establish mechanisms for the continued assessment and improvement of team training | • Guideline 41. Update team training in response to team training evaluation results<br>• Guideline 42. Establish and implement a plan to continue team training and monitor its impact over time<br>• Guideline 43. Continue to assess team training needs in light of organizational goals |
| | Principle 13: Provide opportunities to foster continual team improvement | • Guideline 44. Conduct team training debriefings organized around key events and learning objectives<br>• Guideline 45. Provide opportunities for trainees to use trained teamwork skills on the job<br>• Guideline 46. Provide feedback regarding trainees' use of trained teamwork skills on the job |
| | Principle 14: Motivate and facilitate the long-term transfer and sustainment of teamwork behaviors | • Guideline 47. Support a constant flow of communication by encouraging trainees to voice questions or comments regarding the appropriate use of trained teamwork skills<br>• Guideline 48. Establish a climate in the workplace that encourages the use of trained teamwork skills<br>• Guideline 49. Continue to encourage leadership and management to reinforce and model desired teamwork behaviors<br>• Guideline 50. Implement rewards and consequences for the use/lack of use of trained teamwork skills<br>• Guideline 51. Supply trainees with the resources they need to maintain trained teamwork skills over time |

# References

Allen, N. J., & Hecht, T. D. (2004). The "romance of teams": Toward an understanding of its psychological underpinnings and implications. *Journal of Occupational and Organizational Psychology, 77*, 439–461.

Blickensderfer, E., Cannon-Bowers, J. A., & Salas, E. (1997). Theoretical bases for team-self correction: Fostering shared mental models. In M. M. Beyerlein, D. A. Johnson, & S. T. Beyerlein (Eds.), *Advances in interdisciplinary studies of work teams* (4th ed., pp. 249–279). Greenwich, CT: JAI Press.

Buller, P. F. (1986). The team building-task performance relation: Some conceptual and methodological refinements. *Group & Organization Management, 11*(3), 147–168.

Bush, G. P., & Hattery, L. H. (1956). Teamwork and creativity in research. *Administrative Science Quarterly, 1*(3), 361–372.

Dyer, J. L. (1984). Review on team training and performance: A state-of-the-art review. In F. A. Muckler, A. S. Neal, & L. Strother (Eds.), *Human factors review* (pp. 285–323). Santa Monica, CA: Human Factors Society.

Gladstein, D. L. (1984). Groups in context: A model of task group effectiveness. *Administrative Science Quarterly, 29*, 499–517.

Gregory, M. E., Feitosa, J., Driskell, T., & Salas, E. (2013). Designing, delivering, and evaluating training in organizations: Principles that work. In E. Salas, S. I. Tannenbaum, D. Cohen, & G. Latham (Eds.), *Developing and enhancing teamwork in organizations: Evidence-based best practices and guidelines* (pp. 441–487). San Francisco, CA: Jossey-Bass.

Guzzo, R., & Dickson, M. W. (1996). Team in organizations: Recent research on performance and effectiveness. *Annual Review of Psychology, 47*, 307–338.

Hackman, J. R. (1987). The design of work teams. In J.W. Lorsch (Ed.), *Handbook of organizational behavior* (pp. 315–342). Englewood Cliffs, NJ: Prentice Hall.

Hackman, J. R. (1998). Why teams don't work. In R. S. Tindale, L. Heath, & J. Edwards (Eds.), *Theory and research on small groups* (pp. 246–267). New York, NY: Plenum Press.

Kozlowski, S.W.J., & Bell, B. S. (2003). Work groups and teams in organizations. In W. C. Borman, D. R. Ilgen, & R. J. Klimoski (Eds.), *Handbook of psychology* (pp. 333–375). Hoboken, NJ: John Wiley & Sons.

Kozlowski, S.W.J., & Ilgen, D. R. (2006). Enhancing the effectiveness of work groups and teams. *Psychological Science in the Public Interest, 7*(3), 77–124.

Kraiger, K., Ford, J. K., & Salas, E. (1993). Application of cognitive, skill-based, and affective theories of learning outcomes to new methods of training evaluation. *Journal of Applied Psychology, 78*(2), 311–328.

LePine, J. A., Piccolo, R. F., Jackson, C. L., Mathieu, J. E., & Saul, J. R. (2008). A meta-analysis of teamwork processes: Tests of a multidimensional model and relationships with team effectiveness criteria. *Personnel Psychology, 61*, 273–307.

Marks, M. A., Mathieu, J. E., & Zaccaro, J. (2001). A temporally based framework and taxonomy of team processes. *The Academy of Management Review, 26*(3), 356–376.

Molenda, M., Reigeluth, C. M., & Nelson, L. M. (2003). Instructional design. In L. Nadel (Ed.), *Encyclopedia of cognitive science* (pp. 574–578). London, UK: Nature Publishing Group.

Moreland, R. L., Argote, L., Krishnan, R. (2002). Training people to work in groups. *Theory and Research on Small Groups, 4*, 37–60.

Moreland, R. L., & Levine, J. M. (1992). The composition of small groups. In E. J. Lawler, B. Markovsky, & H. A. Walker (Eds.), *Advances in Group Processes* (pp. 237–280). Greenwich, CT: JAI Press.

Rosen, M. A., Salas, E., Silvestri, S., Wu, T., & Lazzara, E. H. (2008). A measurement tool for simulation-based training in emergency medicine: The simulation module for assessment of resident targeted event responses (SMARTER) approach. *Simulation in Healthcare, 3*(3), 170–179.

Saavendra, R., Earley, P. C., & Van Dyne, L. (1993). Complex interdependence in task-performing groups. *Journal of Applied Psychology, 78*(1), 61–72.

Salas, E., & Cannon-Bowers, J. A. (2000). The anatomy of team training. In S. Tobias & J. D. Fletcher (Eds.), *Training & retraining: A handbook for business, industry, and government* (pp. 312–335). New York, NY: Macmillan Reference USA.

Salas, E., & Cannon-Bowers, J. A. (2001). The science of training: A decade of progress. *Annual Review of Psychology, 52,* 471–499.

Salas, E., DiazGranados, D., Klein, C., Burke, C. S., Stagl, K. C., Goodwin, G. F., & Halpin, S.M. (2008). Does team training improve team performance? A meta-analysis. *Human Factors, 50*(6), 903–933.

Salas, E., Dickenson, T. L., Converse, S. A., & Tannenbaum, S. I. (1992). Toward an understanding of team performance and training. In R. J. Swezey & E. Salas (Eds.), *Teams: Their training and performance* (pp. 3–29). Norwood, NJ: Ablex.

Salas, E., Rosen, M.A., Burke, C. S., & Goodwin, G. F. (2009). The wisdom of collectives in organizations: An update of the teamwork competencies. In E. Salas, G. F. Goodwin, & C. S. Burke (Eds.), *Team effectiveness in complex organizations: Cross-disciplinary perspectives and approaches* (pp. 39–79). New York, NY: Taylor & Francis.

Salas, E., Rozell, D., Mullen, B., & Driskell, J. E. (1999). The effect of team building on performance: An integration. *Small Group Research, 30*(3), 309–329.

Shuffler, M. L., Burke, C.S., Kramer, W. S., & Salas, E. (2012). Leading teams: Past, present, and future. In M.G. Rumsey (Ed.), *The Oxford handbook of leadership* (pp. 144–166). New York, NY: Oxford University Press.

Stagl, K. C., Burke, C. S., Salas, E., & Pierce, L. (2006). Team adaptation: Realizing team synergy. In C. S. Burke, L. G. Pierce, & E. Salas (Eds.), *Advances in human performance and cognitive engineering research* (Vol. 6, pp. 117–141). Elsevier.

Sundstrom, E., DeMeuse, K. P., & Futrell, D. (1990). Work teams: Applications and effectiveness. *American Psychologist, 45,* 120–133.

Swezey, R. W., & Salas, E. (1992). Guidelines for use in team-training development. In R. W. Swezey & E. Salas, E. (Eds.), *Teams: Their training and performance* (pp. 219–245). Westport, CT: Ablex.

Tannenbaum, S. I., Beard, R. L., & Salas, E. (1992). Team building and its influence on team effectiveness: An examination of conceptual and empirical developments. *Advances in Psychology, 82,* 117–153.

Woodman, R.W., & Sherwood, J.J. (1980). The role of team development in organizational effectiveness: A critical review. *Psychological Bulletin, 88*(1), 166–186.

Wuchty, S., Jones, B. F., & Uzzi, B. (2007). The increasing dominance of teams in production of knowledge. *Science, 316,* 1036–1039.

# 2

## PILLAR 1

Ensure the Need for Teamwork Behaviors
and Team Training

Performance "problems" are "symptoms" of a deeper "illness." Root causes must be identified before selecting an intervention.

**Is team training always the answer?** Not necessarily. Just as doctors prescribe different medicines for varying ailments, different interventions are needed for different organizational problems. Team training cannot *always* be this medicine. Again, just as in medicine, the first, most critical step is to get to the bottom of the problem, so that a proper diagnosis can be made. For example, the problem may not be the inability to do a job, but it may be the unwillingness to do a job. After identifying the symptom (e.g., an increased accident rate over the past year), it is essential to ascertain the underlying "sickness" that is causing the symptoms. In this case, it could be that employees are using poorly maintained equipment, which is causing the accidents. Or, it may be that employees do not have the safety knowledge and teamwork skills necessary to engage in safe practices. Only in the latter of these two scenarios would team training be necessary.

Team training allows the organization to teach employees proper safety protocols and the team skills and behaviors needed to safely perform their tasks. Beyond simply assuring that team training will be relevant for the root cause of the problem, to increase the likelihood that team training will be successful, it is critical to identify who will be trained (existing employees, new employees, a mixture of both?), the knowledge and skills they currently have, and the knowledge and skills they need to have to perform successfully. Returning to the safety example, it may be that only a small subset of employees are responsible for the increase in accident rates. Analysis of the situation, for example, could reveal consistent communication breakdowns between these individuals—in this instance, not *every* employee would need to be trained, and even of this subset, they may not need to be trained on *every* safety protocol or *every* single element of teamwork. Identify what is wrong, and provide a targeted intervention, rather than wasting time and resources with a buckshot approach.

In this chapter, we outline strategies for identifying whether team training is an appropriate solution to improve performance. In doing so, we specify two principles: (1) collect the necessary data and (2) evaluate whether team training should be pursued as an improvement strategy.

## Principle 1: Systematically Identify Characteristics of the Organization, Team Tasks, and Individual Team Members[1]

In order to establish the need for teamwork behaviors, it is first necessary to identify relevant characteristics of the organization, team tasks, and individual team members. Collecting data on these elements is the core of a team training needs analysis (TTNA); this process provides essential information to inform whether team training is needed and elicits the resource requirements needed to accomplish team training goals. Additionally, the TTNA provides a systematic approach to help determine the goals and objectives of a team training program (see Chapter 4). This makes the TTNA a critical first step for any training endeavor. It yields valuable information to help ensure team members will actually be trained on relevant competencies as well as indicate factors that may facilitate or impede the design and implementation of team training. For further discussion on how to translate team training needs into team training goals, objectives, and implementation solutions, see Chapter 4.

### Guideline 1: Determine How Organizational Factors (e.g., Culture, Climate, Strategic Goals) May Facilitate or Hinder Teamwork[2]

One component of the TTNA is an organizational analysis. An organizational analysis is conducted to establish the organizational components (e.g., climate, norms about expected behavior), strategic goals, resources, and constraints that may affect how the team training program is delivered. Identifying possible barriers prior to team training implementation can help ensure team training goals are realized; constraints that may stymie team training success can be classified and remedied (Salas & Cannon-Bowers, 2001).

This analysis will also help inform whether elements of the **organizational climate** (e.g., managerial support) will support or constrain the implementation, transfer, and maintenance of team training. Additionally, the TTNA should determine to what extent the stated objectives of training

**Organizational Climate:** The environment of the organization, its priorities and values, and the practices and norms of trainers and employees.

are supported by and supportive of organizational factors (see Chapters 3, 4, and 6). For example, Tracey, Tannenbaum, and Kavanagh (1995) investigated how attributes of the organizational context influenced how well supervisory skills learned during training transferred to the job for supermarket managers. Specifically, the effective transfer of trained behaviors (e.g., problem solving, decision making, communication) was affected by organizational climate factors such as performance feedback systems, degree of social support, and whether the organization had a culture of continuous learning. Being aware of potentially harmful climate elements allows the team trainer to either preemptively address these problems or temper the client's expectations.

Organizational analysis should focus on identifying information that will shed light on strategic requirements and external factors that may facilitate or impede team training (Salas, Tannenbaum, Kraiger, & Smith-Jentsch, 2012). Identifying this information can be accomplished by conducting interviews with managers and staff, reviewing relevant organizational documentation, and reviewing existing team training materials. Tips and advice for conducting an organizational analysis are provided in the table below.

---

## TIPS AND ADVICE

- Use employee interviews, focus groups, and surveys to gather information.
    o Require organizational leadership to define the organization's goals and mission statement.
    o Ask employees to describe what they commonly believe is emphasized and valued within the organization (i.e., what is the culture?).
    o Encourage employees to share how they feel at work and why (i.e., what is the climate?).
    o Delve into questions about what employees understand to be appropriate and expected behavior within their organization (i.e., what are the norms?).
- Read available organizational records and documentation (e.g., written rules and regulations, standard operating procedures, the company website, and previous or existing training documentation) that can provide insight into characteristics of the organization.
- Evaluate whether organizational factors represent barriers to effective teamwork and whether the organization has taken steps to remediate these issues.
    o Seek input from employees about what specific aspects of the organization make it difficult to engage in teamwork.

o Consider whether common threats to teamwork (e.g., lack of leadership support, job stressors) are present within the organization.

o Extract trends from employee interviews, focus groups, and surveys.

- Identify whether existing team training programs or supporting systems (e.g., job aids, organizational policies) have fostered or impeded teamwork.

- Define the organization's goals, structure, operational environment, and strategic objectives.

Adapted from: Aguinis & Kraiger, 2009; Goldstein & Ford, 2002; Kraiger & Culbertson, 2013; Noe, 2002; Salas & Stagl, 2009.

## Guideline 2: Define the Team's Purpose and What Teamwork Competencies (i.e., Knowledge, Skills, and Attitudes [KSAs]) Are Required to Achieve Team Goals[3]

The second component of the TTNA is the team task analysis. The team task analysis consists of identifying the operational tasks (i.e., taskwork) as well as the teamwork (e.g., communication, coordination, cooperation) behaviors essential for effective team performance. Taskwork is necessary but not sufficient for effective team performance. For teams to be successful, they must be able to effectively perform both taskwork and teamwork skills (Glickman et al., 1987). Therefore, it is necessary to identify the task skills and teamwork skills required to accomplish team goals in a smooth, coordinated manner. The team task analysis can be thought of as the "blueprint" for team training design, implementation, and evaluation (Salas et al., 2012). Information from the team task analysis will help inform what needs to be trained (see Chapter 4) and explicates how performance should be measured to evaluate team training success (see Chapter 5) (Smith-Jentsch, Salas, & Cannon-Bowers, 2006).

The first step in conducting the team task analysis is to identify the specific jobs or tasks that require teamwork. Upon identifying these, essential components must be described, including work functions of the job and the resources needed (e.g., materials, equipment). After identifying the jobs, their functions, and resources, key task requirements must be determined. That is, what are the teamwork and taskwork KSAs needed for effective team performance? (See Appendix 1 for a listing of possibly relevant teamwork KSAs.) Finally, task specifications—such as job conditions and quality/performance expectations—should be identified. Together, these help the team trainer (or training developer) assess *what* exactly needs to be trained, *who* needs to be trained, and *how much* training needs to be delivered.

One way to conduct a TTNA is to design and execute a controlled experiment. This affords the training developer a great degree of control and should greatly increase confidence that the findings of the TTNA are accurate. Unfortunately, controlled experiments are very resource intensive and often difficult to coordinate. To illustrate, consider the attention to detail that would be required to conduct a controlled TTNA experiment to uncover the teamwork behaviors essential for flight crew performance. Bowers, Jentsch, Salas, and Braun (1998) did just this when they studied communication sequences in simulated flight tasks. They were concerned with identifying the communication patterns that differentiate high-performing from low-performing teams with the end goal being to develop a team training program for more effective communication. The researchers required pilots to complete a simulated reconnaissance mission under unique conditions that would test aspects of their teamwork and communication. Specific communication behaviors were identified by the researchers and measured, including: uncertainty statements, action statements (i.e., those directing another crew member to perform a task), acknowledgements, (i.e., confirming a message), planning statements, factual statements (i.e., verbally stating information about simulation events), nontask-related statements, and statements directed to air traffic control. Compared to simply analyzing the *frequency* and *content* of communication (i.e., what is being said and by whom), the authors demonstrated that it is also important to understand the *sequence* in which communication occurs. For example, higher-performing teams repeated commands more than once and repeated them rapidly compared to lower-performing teams, which simply repeated the command once. Higher-performing teams were also more likely to make planning statements following communications with air traffic control. This admittedly complex process can nonetheless help team training developers generate explicit hypotheses about the factors that contribute to effective team performance, ultimately leading to a more targeted and effective training program.

In some situations however, conducting a controlled experiment as part of the TTNA may not be practical or even necessary. For instance, subject matter expert interviews may be a more feasible and realistic alternative. Appendix 2 outlines possible questions to ask during such an interview. To this end, it is important for team training developers to construct a model of what the expert team members know (Cooke, 1999) in order to determine what KSAs are needed to perform a task. Interviewing high-performing team members and other subject matter experts also enables the team training developer to identify the cues and strategies that facilitate a team member's decision to apply the appropriate skills, which may ultimately become an emphasis in the training itself (Salas & Cannon-Bowers, 2001).

## TIPS AND ADVICE

- Use employee interviews, focus groups, and surveys to gather information (see Appendix 2 for example interview questions).
  - o Ask employees to explain how they work in teams, what they find most challenging about teamwork, and what they need to know, be able to do, and feel in order for the team to be effective.
  - o Gather information about what team tasks are most important, frequent, and difficult.
- Be hands on.
  - o Observe teams in action.
  - o Perform team tasks if appropriate.
- Review organizational documentation (e.g., standard operating procedures, incident reports, skill inventories, task listings) related to team requirements and goals.
- Using the information you gathered, decide what competencies are necessary for effective teamwork.
  - o Rely on scientific literature to identify KSAs that are known to be important; this can guide what you initially assess.
  - o Extract trends from employee interviews, focus groups, and surveys.
  - o Identify which teamwork competencies are most lacking and/or susceptible to decay over time.
- Differentiate between what constitutes expert and novice team performance.
  - o Identify variations in how expert teams work to achieve task objectives compared to novice teams (e.g., problem-solving and communication strategies).
  - o Explicate team member roles and responsibilities for each task.
  - o Identify communication and coordination requirements.
- Determine whether required teamwork competencies are context driven (i.e., team specific, task specific), team contingent (i.e., team specific, task generic), task contingent (team generic, task specific), or transportable (i.e., team generic, task generic).
- Identify the degree to which teams need to coordinate with other entities (both inside and outside the organization).

Adapted from: Cannon-Bowers, Tannenbaum, Salas, & Volpe, 1995; Kraiger, 2003; Mathieu & Tesluk, 2010; Oser, Cannon-Bowers, Salas, & Dwyer, 1999; Salas & Cannon-Bowers, 2000b.

## Guideline 3: Understand the Individual Characteristics Likely to Impact Teamwork and Team Training[4]

The last component of the TTNA is a person analysis. Person analysis involves identifying the individual characteristics likely to impact teamwork and team training. It also helps pinpoint which employees would most likely benefit from team training to ensure that the people who need team training will receive it. For instance, do certain team members have the necessary KSAs required for team tasks (see Guideline 2)? As described by Salas and colleagues (2012), limited resources may preclude participation in team training for every person or every team in an organization. Accordingly, determining which individuals (e.g., only pilots out of an entire flight crew) or teams (e.g., only a surgical team out of an entire hospital unit) that are most in need of team training will ensure that those most in need of training will receive it.

Individual characteristics, such as motivation and learning preferences, can also influence the success of team training. For instance, cognitive ability, age, self-efficacy, and personality factors have been shown to influence the motivation for and effectiveness of training (Colquitt, Lepine, & Noe, 2000). This suggests that not all learners will benefit equally from training opportunities (Sims, Burke, Metcalf, & Salas, 2008). For example, Colquitt and colleagues (2000) reported that older learners were less motivated to train, did not learn as much, and were not as confident in their ability to apply trained skills. This means mechanisms should be introduced to improve the team training experience for older learners. Evaluation of these individual difference variables should take place *before* team training begins because they should shape the development of team training content and material. For instance, the design of certain team training delivery mechanisms (e.g., technology) can be used to make the team training environment more engaging for learners, thereby fostering trainee motivation and interest in team training content (see Chapters 3 and 4).

---

### TIPS AND ADVICE

- Consider team members' prior experience, proficiency, and training history.
    - o Determine if certain individuals need team training more than others because their responsibilities require the use of teamwork competencies, or because they are in need of accreditation/certification.
    - o Prioritize those with the least amount of experience and proficiency.
- Assess individual characteristics such as motivation, commitment, and learning preferences; these characteristics can influence learning and transfer.

Adapted from: Colquitt et al., 2000; Salas & Stagl, 2009.

## Principle 2: Evaluate Whether the Organization Is Ready to Receive Team Training[5]

As described earlier in the chapter, team training may not be the solution to all performance problems. The purpose of TTNA is to systematically identify information about: (1) the organization, (2) tasks the team performs, and (3) the team members themselves in order to establish the need for teamwork behaviors and specifically what kind of team training is needed in the organization. A next step for team training developers is to evaluate whether the organization is *ready* to receive team training. This is accomplished by determining whether teamwork deficiencies are the root cause of organization problems, confirming that team training is the most appropriate solution to redress team performance deficiencies, and ensuring that the organization can adequately support the team training endeavor.

### Guideline 4: Analyze the Cause of Performance Deficiencies and Consider Appropriate Improvement Strategies[6]

The outcome of Principle 1 should provide the evidence required to determine if team training is needed to improve performance outcomes. For example, when conducting the TTNA, training developers might come to learn that teams don't always have all of the information they need to successfully complete a task. But is this information that team members need to know/have memorized (e.g., a knowledge component), or might it be reasonably accessed with better job aids (Salas et al., 2012)? Illustrative of the former is an awareness of team members' roles and responsibilities. This knowledge is a trainable KSA essential to daily team functioning. If team members do not demonstrate an appropriate understanding of this knowledge domain, team training focused on improving this knowledge gap would be appropriate. On the other hand, if the training needs analysis reveals a knowledge gap due to information being scattered across an array of information repositories and systems (and this knowledge is not essential on a daily basis), team training aimed at enabling team members to memorize every piece of task-relevant information would not be practical. The cognitive burden involved in memorization and information retrieval can entail considerable time to train team members to demonstrate an ability that they adequately know and are able to process information. Instead, developing job aids such as knowledge repositories, checklists, and other information retrieval strategies may be a better solution than investing team training resources (Salas et al., 2012). Determining the nature of the deficient KSA will guide whether the organization should offer team training, improve the nature or availability of their job aids, or provide some other intervention.

---

### TIPS AND ADVICE

- Define the problem and ascertain whether teamwork is the root cause.
- Evaluate whether the current level of teamwork meets organizational goals and expectations.
  - o Consider the differences between what constitutes expert and novice team performance (see Guideline 2).
  - o Leverage the information gathered from subject matter experts, organizational documentation, and observations (refer to Guidelines 1 and 2) to establish the need for improved teamwork within the organization.
- Identify whether needed areas of improvement represent behaviors (e.g., coordination), attitudes (e.g., cohesion), or cognitions (e.g., shared situational awareness) (refer to Guideline 2).
- Consider alternative solutions to team training (e.g., job aids, additional staffing) for improving teamwork.

Adapted from: Brown & Sitzmann, 2011; Salas & Cannon-Bowers, 1997; Salas & Cannon-Bowers, 2000a; Salas et al., 2012.

---

### Guideline 5: Determine Whether the Organization Can Adequately Support Team Training[7]

Guideline 5 can best be conceptualized as an extension of Guidelines 1 and 3. These guidelines illustrate how training developers can identify attributes of the organization and of the learner that are likely to influence team training success. For example, Tracey and colleagues (1995) investigated the influence of organizational factors on training effectiveness. They found that when employees believed that their work was important and meaningful, they tended to be more motivated and invested in training even before training began. Similarly, they found a significant relationship between the work environment and pre-training self-efficacy and pre-training motivation. In other words, a supportive work environment helped learners to go into the training with a positive attitude that in turn yielded a more effective training regimen. Equipped with this kind of information regarding the individual and organizational influencing factors on team training, team training developers can ultimately assess whether the organization can adequately support team training. (Alonso et al., 2006). For example, do managers send positive messages about the value of team training (see Guideline 6 to see how best to champion the importance of team training)? Are systems in place to prepare and motivate the learner (see Principle 4)? If the answers to questions such as these are "no," then potential barriers to team training have been identified and must be addressed.

Similarly, team training developers must ensure the organization is logistically prepared for team training. This may entail assurance that the organization has sufficient funding to finance team training, that there is dedicated training time and space, and that employees can fit team training into their work schedule. As noted by Salas, Weaver, and Shuffler (2012), not all training needs share the same level of significance. If limitations to organizational resources preclude the adoption of all team training objectives, team training can be prioritized based on the most important strategic/organizational needs that were identified from the training needs analysis in relation to available resources.

---

## TIPS AND ADVICE

- Take stock of stakeholders' opinions regarding team training.
    - o Determine if management supports the team training endeavor.
    - o Determine if the importance of team training has been communicated by management to workers (see also Principle 3).
- Find out if the organization has resources available to conduct team training (e.g., financial support, space, materials, time, personnel).
- Outline team training priorities in light of strategic objectives and team training resources.

Adapted from: Aguinis & Kraiger, 2009; Lazzara, Benishek, Dietz, Salas, & Adriansen, 2014; Noe, 2002; Salas et al., 2012.

---

## Notes

1 Goldstein & Ford, 2002; Kraiger, 2003; Noe, 2002; Salas, Tannenbaum, Kraiger, & Smith-Jentsch, 2012; Salas & Stagl, 2009; Salas, Weaver, & Shuffler, 2012; Surface, 2012; Wilson, 2005
2 Noe, 2002; Quiñones, 1997; Salas et al., 2008
3 Arthur, Edwards, Bell, Villado, & Bennett, 2005; Arthur et al., 2012; Baker, Salas, & Cannon-Bowers, 1998; Cannon-Bowers, Tannenbaum, Salas, & Volpe, 1995; Salas & Rosen, 2008
4 Colquitt, LePine, & Noe, 2000; Mathieu & Martineau, 1997
5 Brown, 2002; Goldstein & Ford, 2002; Salas & Cannon-Bowers, 2000a; Salas, Wilson, Burke, Wightman, & Howse, 2006; Salas et al., 2008
6 Noe, 2002; Salas et al., 2012; Surface, 2012
7 Klein, Sims, & Salas, 2006; Salas, Wilson-Donnelly, Sims, Burke, & Priest, 2007

## References

Aguinis, H., & Kraiger, K. (2009). Benefits of training and development for individuals and teams, organizations, and society. *Annual Review of Psychology, 60,* 451–474.

Alonso, A., Baker, D., Holtzman, A., Day, R., King, H., Toomey, L., & Salas, E. (2006). Reducing medical error in the Military Health System: How can team training help? *Human Resource Management Review, 16*(3), 396–415.

Arthur, W., Edwards, B. D., Bell, S. T., Villado, A. J., & Bennett, W. (2005). Team task analysis: Identifying tasks and jobs that are team based. *Human Factors, 47*(3), 654–669.

Arthur, W., Glaze, R. M., Bhupatkar, A., Villado, A. J., Bennett, W., & Rowe, L. J. (2012). Team task analysis: Differentiating between tasks using team relatedness and team workflow as metrics of team task interdependence. *Human Factors, 54*(2), 277–295.

Baker, D., Salas, E., & Cannon-Bowers, J. (1998). Team job analysis: A critical training need? In *Proceedings of the human factors and ergonomics society 42nd annual meeting* (pp. 1408–1411). Santa Monica, CA: Human Factors and Ergonomics Society.

Bowers, C., Jentsch, F., Salas, E., & Braun, C. (1998). Analyzing communication sequences for team training needs assessment. *Human Factors, 40*(4), 672–679.

Brown, J. (2002). Training needs assessment: A must for developing an effective training program. *Public Personnel Management, 31*(4), 569–578.

Brown, K.G., & Sitzmann, T. (2011). Training and employee development for improved performance. In S. Zedeck (Ed.), *APA handbook of industrial and organizational psychology: Vol. 2 Selecting and developing members for the organization* (pp. 469–503). Washington, DC: American Psychological Association.

Cannon-Bowers, J., Tannenbaum, S., Salas, E., & Volpe, C. (1995). Defining competencies and establishing team training requirements. *Team Effectiveness and Decision Making in Organizations, 1,* 333–380.

Colquitt, J., LePine, J., & Noe, R. (2000). Toward an integrative theory of training motivation: A meta-analytic path analysis of 20 years of research. *Journal of Applied Psychology, 85*(5), 678–707.

Cooke, N. J. (1999). Knowledge elicitation. In F. Durso (Eds.), *Handbook of applied cognition* (pp. 479–509). Chichester, UK: Wiley.

Goldstein, I. L., & Ford, J.K. (2002). *Training in organizations* (4th ed.). Belmont, CA: Wadsworth.

Glickman, A. S., Zimmer, S., Montero, R. C., Guerette, P. J., Campbell, W. J., Morgan Jr., B. B., & Salas, E. (1987). The evolution of team skills: An empirical assessment with implications for training (NTSC 87–016). Arlington, VA: Office of Naval Research.

Klein, C., Sims, D. E., & Salas, E. (2006). Training evaluation. In W. Karwowski (Ed.), *International encyclopedia of ergonomics and human factors* (2nd ed., pp. 2434–2439). Boca Raton, FL: CRC Press.

Kraiger K. (2003). Perspectives on training and development. In W. C. Borman, D.R. Ilgen, & R.J. Klimoski (Eds.), *Handbook of psychology: Vol. 12 Industrial and organizational psychology* (pp. 171–192). Hoboken, NJ: John Wiley & Sons.

Kraiger, K., & Culbertson, S.S. (2013). Understanding and facilitating learning: Advancements in training and development. In N.W. Schmitt, S. Highhouse, I.B. Weiner (Eds.), *Handbook of psychology: Vol. 12 Industrial and organizational psychology* (2nd ed., pp. 244–261). Hoboken, NJ: John Wiley & Sons.

Lazzara, E. H., Benishek, L. E., Dietz, A.S., Salas, E., & Adriansen, D. J. (2014). Eight critical factors in creating and implementing a successful simulation program. *The Joint Commission Journal on Quality and Patient Safety, 40*(1), 21–29.

Mathieu, J.E., & Martineau, J.W. (1997). Individual and situational influences in training motivation. In J.K. Ford & Associates (Eds.), *Improving training effectiveness in work organizations* (pp. 193–222). Mahwah, NJ: Lawrence Erlbaum Associates.

Mathieu, J.E., & Tesluk, P.E. (2010). A multilevel perspective on training and development effectiveness. In S.J. Kozlowski & E. Salas (Eds.), *Learning, training, and development in organizations* (pp. 405–440). New York, NY: Routledge/Taylor & Francis Group.

Noe, R.A. (2002). *Employee training and development* (2nd ed.). Boston, MA: McGraw-Hill/Irwin.

Oser, R., Cannon-Bowers, J., Salas, E., & Dwyer, D. (1999). Enhancing human performance in technology-rich environments: Guidelines for scenario-based training. In E. Salas (Ed.), *Human/Technology interaction in complex systems* (pp. 175–202). Greenwich, CT: JAI Press.

Quiñones, M.A. (1997). Contextual influence on training effectiveness. In M.A. Quiñones & A. Ehrenstein (Eds.), *Training for a rapidly changing workplace* (pp. 177–200). Washington, DC: APA Books.

Salas, E., & Cannon-Bowers, J.A. (1997). Methods, tools, and strategies for team training. In M.A. Quiñones & A. Ehrenstein (Eds.), *Training for a rapidly changing workplace: Applications of psychological research* (pp. 249–279). Washington, DC: APA Books.

Salas, E., & Cannon-Bowers, J. A. (2000a). Design training systematically. In E.A. Locke (Ed.), *Principles of organizational behavior* (pp. 43–59). Oxford, UK: Blackwell.

Salas, E., & Cannon-Bowers, J. A. (2000b). The anatomy of team training. In S. Tobias & J. D. Fletcher (Eds.), *Training & retraining: A handbook for business, industry, and government* (pp. 312–335). New York, NY: Macmillan Reference USA.

Salas, E., & Cannon-Bowers, J. A. (2001). The science of training: A decade of progress. *Annual Review of Psychology, 52*(1), 471–499.

Salas, E., & Rosen, M. A. (2008). Beyond the bells and whistles: When simulation-based team training works best. *CRICO RMF Forum, 26*(4), 6–7.

Salas, E., & Stagl, K. C. (2009). Design training systematically and follow the science of training. In E. A. Locke (Ed.), *Handbook of principles of organizational behavior: Indispensable knowledge for evidence-based management* (2nd ed., pp. 59–84). Chichester, UK: John Wiley & Sons.

Salas, E., Tannenbaum, S., Kraiger, K., & Smith-Jentsch, K. (2012). The science of training and development in organizations: What matters in practice. *Psychological Science in the Public Interest, 13*(2), 74–101.

Salas, E., Weaver, S.J., & Shuffler, M.L. (2012). Learning, training, and development in organizations. In S.J. Kozlowski (Ed.), *The Oxford handbook of organizational psychology* (Vol. 1, pp. 330–372). New York, NY: Oxford University Press.

Salas, E., Wilson, K., Burke, C., Wightman, D., & Howse, W. (2006). A checklist for crew resource management training. *Ergonomics in Design, 2*, 6–15.

Salas, E., Wilson, K., Lazzara, E., King, H., Augenstein, J., Robinson, D., & Birnbach, D. (2008). Simulation-based training for patient safety: 10 principles that matter. *Journal of Patient Safety, 4*(1), 3–8.

Salas, E., Wilson-Donnelly, K.A., Sims, D. E., Burke, C. S., & Priest, H.A. (2007). Teamwork training for patient safety: Best practices and guiding principles. In C. Pascale (Ed.), *Handbook of human factors and ergonomics in healthcare and patient safety* (pp. 803–822). Mahwah, NJ: Lawrence Erlbaum Associates.

Sims, D., Burke, C., Metcalf, D., & Salas, E. (2008). Research-based guidelines for designing blended learning. *Ergonomics in Design, 16*(1), 23–29.

Smith-Jentsch, K. A., Salas, E., & Cannon-Bowers, J. A. (2006). Principles and strategies for team training. In W. Karwowski (Ed.), *International encyclopedia of ergonomics and human factors* (2nd ed., pp. 2245–2248). Boca Raton, FL: CRC Press.

Surface, E. A. (2012). Training needs assessment: Aligning learning and capability with performance requirements and organizational objectives. In M. A. Wilson, W. Bennett, S. G. Gibson, & G. M. Alliger (Eds.), *The handbook of work analysis: Methods, systems, applications, and science of work measurement in organizations* (pp. 437–462). New York, NY: Routledge.

Tracey, J., Tannenbaum, S., & Kavanagh, M. (1995). Applying trained skills on the job: The importance of the work environment. *Journal of Applied Psychology, 80*(2), 239–252.

Wilson, J. P. (Ed.). (2005). *Human resource development: Learning & training for individuals & organizations*. London, UK: Kogan Page Publishers.

# 3

# PILLAR 2

## Create a Positive Team Training Climate for Learning and the Learner

**You've determined that team training is the answer—now what?** If team training is something that can be designed and delivered, it follows that it also has to have a place that it can

> Team training is only as effective as the foundation upon which it is laid.

be *delivered to*. The recipients of training, nested within their organization, are the "delivery spot." One role of the training developer and/or team trainer is to ensure that the delivery spot is optimally prepared to receive team training. How can one ensure such a seamless delivery?

To answer this question, it is helpful to conceptualize team training as any other performance situation, where performance is broadly determined by an individual's *motivation, ability*, and *opportunity*. Each of these variables is essential to successful performance in nearly any situation, and team training is no different. If learners are not motivated to learn, participate in the training, or apply the training, then team training will have little (if any) effect—even if learners are provided with an opportunity to learn. On the other hand, if learners are highly motivated to learn about teams and teamwork behaviors, but do not have (1) the cognitive ability to engage with or learn from the training (e.g., it is too hard) or (2) sufficient opportunities to participate in this training (e.g., it is poorly timed or too time consuming), the intervention will similarly have minimal levels of effectiveness. All three factors are essential for team training to work.

Motivation for team training is a fairly straightforward concept—learners should (1) want to learn, (2) believe that learning will yield desirable outcomes, and (3) believe that training will lead to the learning necessary to achieve the desirable outcomes. By ensuring that learners are motivated to participate in the learning process, trainers can be more certain that learners will actively engage in and learn from the process.

> Without organizational support, learners will not perceive the team training as important.

What is meant by saying that learners must have the opportunity and ability to learn? To explain this, it is essential to understand that team training learners are nested within two social environments: (1) the broader organization and (2) the teams (or groups of individuals) with whom they are being trained. The broader organization offers learners the opportunity to learn. Minimally, this refers to management allowing employees the opportunity to attend and participate in training, but it is more than this. The organizational setting forms the context under which learners have the opportunity to apply what they learn in training on the job. If the organization does not actively support the application of what is being trained, learners will not have a legitimate opportunity to develop more than just conceptual head knowledge. This is discussed in Pillar 5 as it relates to the sustainability and maintenance of learned content, but it is relevant to the initial learning climate as well. First, learners will be less likely to participate at all if they believe that the organization is unsupportive of the training. Second, if learners believe that the organization is only marginally supportive of team training, they are less likely to put forth whatever effort is needed to obtain maximum benefit from the training. Trainers and training developers should, therefore, ensure that the organization supports all aspects of team training.

The team training environment itself is another social setting which the trainer can prepare prior to the actual onset of training. The team training setting presents several issues that may affect learners' active engagement with the learning process. As we discuss in greater detail below, learners' holistic perception of training—the **training climate**—has a major impact on the effectiveness of training. Learners' sense of the training climate is one pillar of training effectiveness that, if not addressed, can lead to disengagement, lack of participation, and ultimately, a lack of learning.

> Learners must not only be actively motivated—they must not be dissuaded from participating or applying teamwork skills.

To summarize, we offer a simple analog as a point of reference. Consider learners in a team training intervention as travelers on a journey towards the destination of more effectively engaging in teamwork behaviors. In some circumstances, the immediate team training environment may be uncomfortable, unsafe, or feel interpersonally risky—causing the learner to "put the brakes" on his or her journey towards learning and development. At other times, an unsupportive organizational environment may make it difficult (or appear difficult) for learners to apply the content of team training on the job. In this case, the learner's foot may not be on the brake, but the path to the destination may be hindered with too many roadblocks (e.g., managerial resistance). And even when the foot is off the brake and the roadblocks are removed, the learner will not move until he or she presses the gas pedal—motivation. In other words, the trainer may establish an interpersonally safe training environment and the organization may fully support team training, but training will not be maximally effective until the learner is engaged and motivated to actively participate in and apply the content of training. Ultimately, for team training to "go," trainers and training developers must remove (or reduce) the organizational roadblocks, release learners' within-training social brakes, and press firmly on learners' motivational gas pedal.

## Principle 3: Generate Support from Organizational Leadership[1]

Before beginning the journey towards team training and development, it is imperative that the road is cleared of any potential roadblocks. In any organizational setting, a lack of managerial or leadership support can be a major roadblock. Unsupportive leadership may make it difficult for learners to participate in training or apply what is learned in training to the actual job performance setting (Salas & Cannon-Bowers, 2000a; Salas & Cannon-Bowers, 2000b; Sims, Salas, & Burke, 2005). Similarly, if organizational leaders do not emphasize the importance of training to learners, learners lose a tangible and salient source of motivation (Bunch, 2007).

On the other hand, when organizational leadership actively supports team training, the motivation for and climate of training is significantly bolstered. By modeling and emphasizing the importance of team training to learners, organizational leaders lay the groundwork for learners to approach training with a positive and motivated mindset (Bunch, 2007). Indeed, research has found that when learners perceive their organizations as supporting the end goals of training, the effects of training are stronger and longer-lasting (Cromwell & Kolb, 2004; Lim, Lee, & Nam, 2007).

The endorsement of leadership is essential in creating a positive climate for training due in part to the influential power that leaders hold within organizations (French & Raven, 1959). Less powerful individuals look to more powerful individuals as a source of guidance (French & Raven, 1959; Ho, Rousseau, & Levesque, 2006; Ibarra & Andrews, 1993) in determining the importance of organizational behavior and expectations. The same is true in regards to team training—in the absence of salient organizational support, learners are prone to infer that training is relatively unimportant. Naturally, when learners fail to ascribe importance to team training, the motivation and engagement required for successful learning is absent, leading to ineffective training experiences and outcomes.

Understanding this, we propose (and answer) two essential questions that team trainers and training developers must ask themselves when preparing the training environment:

1.   *How can I earn buy-in from organizational leadership for team training?*
2.   *How should organizational leadership support team training?*

## Guideline 6: Champion the Importance of Team Training to Leadership[2]

> Leaders need to consistently communicate the importance of teamwork and tout the benefits of team training.

As noted, the support of leadership is essential to the effectiveness of most activities within an organization, and team training interventions are no less dependent on this support (Bunch, 2007; Cromwell & Kolb, 2004; Lim et al., 2007). Indeed, because team training is often resource-intensive (e.g., frequently requiring multiple employees to take time out of the normal workday to engage in developmental activities), leadership support may be even more necessary. If leaders do not "buy in" to the need for team training, the support needed to make team training a success will be glaringly absent. Supportive leaders can bolster the effectiveness of and motivation for training by actively allocating resources for training (e.g., time) and communicating the importance of training to others in the organization. To garner this essential support, trainers and training developers must effectively champion the importance of team training to leadership. Below, we provide some tips and advice for how trainers can elicit the necessary support from organizational leadership. Broadly speaking, these tips and advice can be understood and even expanded with a cursory understanding of what motivates people. Though motivation is a huge research field, a rich history of research suggests that three factors that play a large role in individuals' motivation are:

1.   **Valence**—or the desirability of a given outcome.
2.   **Instrumentality**—or how important a given action is in achieving the outcome.
3.   **Expectancy**—or how likely it is that the given action will be successfully completed, leading to the desirable outcome (Mento, Locke, & Klein, 1992; Pritchard & Sanders, 1973; Vroom, 1964).

To apply this to the team training context, consider the following. Trainers should identify what constitutes a desirable outcome for organizational leaders (see Pillar 1). Having identified this, trainers must communicate to organizational leadership how necessary (instrumental) team training is for achieving these outcomes, and how effective the training will be (i.e., how strongly they can expect the training to be effective). By appealing to these three factors of motivation, trainers may gain the support of organizational leadership.

## TIPS AND ADVICE

- Use jargon-free language to explain to leadership the importance of teamwork, and how team training has been shown to improve teamwork.
- Explain to leadership how teamwork is used in their organization and how team training can help improve team performance (see Pillar 1).
- Use multimedia presentation tools (e.g., videos of teams in real performance situations) when necessary to illustrate the importance of teamwork.
- Link team training outcomes to the organization's bottom line.
- Seek leader input throughout the development, delivery, evaluation, and sustainment of team training.
- Identify allies from leadership to champion team training.

Adapted from: Aguinis & Kraiger, 2009; Goldstein & Ford, 2002; Salas & Cannon-Bowers, 2000a.

## Guideline 7: Encourage Leadership to Establish Conditions for Reinforcing and Modeling Desired Teamwork Behaviors Before and During Team Training[3]

Because team training is focused on developing and changing KSAs that are frequently outside the realm of basic task performance, sustainable change and transfer of training to the work environment requires additional attention and effort (i.e., motivation) beyond what is typically required for task performance. One way to facilitate the motivation required for successful learning and transfer of team training is for organizational leaders to not only endorse training verbally or simply allocate resources to team training but to take an active role in supporting learning—both before and during team training.

This support should be done systematically so as to more fully communicate to learners the importance that organizational leadership ascribes to team training (Bunch, 2007). Systematic support and reinforcement of team

> Leaders must set the conditions under which teamwork can flourish.

training means that trainers and leadership collaborate to strategically optimize the quantity and quality of ways in which the importance of team training is communicated. Indeed, organizational leaders may use their position as establishers and communicators of organizational culture to encourage employees' learning and development (Bierly, Kessler, & Christensen, 2000; Egan, Yang, & Bartlett, 2004; Hurley & Hult, 1998). In this guideline, we present various ways in which past research has suggested that trainers and leadership might systematically communicate the importance of team training to learners.

---

**TIPS AND ADVICE**

- Clearly define, clarify, and communicate desired teamwork behaviors to leadership.
- Urge leaders to reward and acknowledge the display of team training KSAs in the workplace.
- Explain how leadership modeling teamwork behaviors reinforces trainees' use of those behaviors (e.g., describe empirical findings).
- Offer team training to leadership and train all organizational stakeholders together when possible.
- Advocate for leaders to attend team training sessions as both attendees and presenters.
- Urge leaders to promote employee attendance at team training sessions.
- Schedule opportunities for organizational leadership to talk to trainees about their support and expectations for team training and teamwork.
- Emphasize the importance of providing standardized, timely, and diagnostic feedback as a mechanism to communicate team training progress and performance.
- Make a business case why teamwork matters.

Adapted from: Goldstein & Ford, 2002; Noe, 2002; Salas & Cannon-Bowers, 2000b.

---

## Principle 4: Prepare and Motivate the Learner for Team Training[4]

Though the support of organizational leadership is essential to facilitating the effectiveness of team training, if learners are not sufficiently motivated to participate in, engage with, and learn from team training, the impact of training will be severely limited. This is because learning is active, not passive, requiring learners to perceive, store, categorize, recall, apply, and adapt the content being taught in team training (Evans, 2008; Prince, 2004). All of these actions require psychological energy and motivation. Absent motivation, learners may not pay attention to or actively participate in training, or they may simply not attend.

If learners perceive team training to be a waste of time—due (for example) to excessive difficulty, coercive obligation, lack of organizational support, or perceived irrelevance—the motivation necessary for successful learning will be absent (Amabile, 1996; Bandura, 1977; Chiaburu & Marinova, 2005; Locke &

Latham, 1990; Locke & Latham, 2002; Locke & Latham, 2006; Locke, Shaw, Saari, & Latham, 1981; Merrian, 2001; Morrell & Korsgaard, 2011; Saks, 1994; Schwoerer, May, Hollensbe, & Mencl, 2005; Tharenou, 2001; Zemke & Zemke, 1984). Conversely, when learners see the relevance, importance, and desirability of training, and the outcomes associated with training (Mento et al., 1992; Pritchard & Sanders, 1973; Vroom, 1964), they are more likely to be sufficiently engaged in the training process (Tharenou, 2001). When learners make this connection, it is a sustainable source of motivational energy, which will increase the likelihood that learners remain engaged throughout the training process.

In addition to the motivating potential of training content (i.e., its valence, instrumentality, and desirability—see Guideline 6), team trainers may facilitate learners' motivation in other ways by appealing to self-efficacy (Bandura, 1977) and utilizing effective goal-setting techniques (Locke & Latham, 1990). That is, trainers may communicate to learners that the training is not overly difficult or resource intensive (increasing self-efficacy), or they may break the training process down into more manageable segments (leveraging the inherently motivational power of specific, measureable, achievable goals). By leveraging the science of motivation theory, team trainers and developers can build motivating elements directly into the environment, design, and delivery of team training. We discuss these various avenues of learner motivation in the guidelines below.

## Guideline 8: Frame Team Training in a Positive Light[5]

Assuming the organization supports the training to the point of making it mandatory, trainers must take care to frame the training in a positive and motivational light. Activities that are obligatory are typically seen as less engaging than those that are optional or voluntary. Generally speak-

> Communicate to learners the message that team training is an opportunity to excel and improve their own jobs and units.

ing, this is because volitional activities are associated with individuals' **intrinsic motivation**; that is, the individuals' inherent motivation and interest in the activity itself (compared to extrinsic motivators such as cash rewards or aversion to punishment). This kind of motivation is typically considered more sustainable (Guay, Vallerand, & Blanchard, 2000; Isen & Reeve, 2005) and is often associated with deeper and more creative thought processes (Amabile, 1996). In this respect, voluntary training may be desirable. However, completely voluntary training may signal to employees that organizational leadership does not actively support team training (Bunch, 2007) and may hinder participation because employees must weigh the pros and cons of participating in training versus the possibility of falling behind in other work responsibilities (Morrell & Korsgaard, 2011).

Accordingly, team trainers and organizational leaders alike must be intentional about communicating the right kind of message about training. When training is presented in a negative light to learners (e.g., as a requirement, a remedial intervention, or a punishment of some sort), the intrinsic motivation conducive to successful training outcomes is severely hampered. Team trainers can circumvent this threat by framing team training positively to learners (and encouraging organizational leadership to communicate a similar message—see Guideline 7). There are several ways in which trainers can frame training in a maximally motivational light. On the whole, the effects of training should be linked to outcomes that are intrinsically desirable to learners. Furthermore, these touted effects should be communicated in such a way that training is seen as an *instrumental* and essential way to achieve the desirable advertised outcomes (Pritchard & Sanders, 1973; Vroom, 1964). We highlight the possible ways for achieving this below.

---

### TIPS AND ADVICE

- Describe team training as an opportunity, not an obligation or a punishment.
- Ensure that teams and individuals perceive team training to be useful and/or necessary.
- Express the value of team training by linking team training to:
    - (1) broader organizational goals.
    - (2) team performance goals.
    - (3) desirable team outcomes such as less conflict.
    - (4) individual goals such as increased job satisfaction.
    - (5) consumer, client, and/or community outcomes.

Adapted From: Axtell, Maitlis, & Yearta (1997); Burke & Hutchins, 2007; Goldstein & Ford, 2002; Noe, 2002; Salas & Cannon-Bowers, 2000b; Tannenbaum, Mathieu, Salas, & Cannon-Bowers, 1991.

---

### Guideline 9: Encourage Trainees to Set Goals Prior to Participating in Team Training[6]

As noted earlier, team training (and more broadly, the learning process in general) requires the learner to be motivated (Evans, 2008; Merrian, 2001; Prince, 2004; Zemke & Zemke, 1984) in the training context. While the content of training can (and certainly should) be motivating to learners, trainers can leverage other motivational techniques to enhance learners' motivation throughout the team training process. One of these techniques is the well-known strategy of goal-setting.

A long tradition of psychological research strongly suggests the motivational power of goals and goal-setting for enhancing individual and team performance, and team trainers can leverage this research to enhance learners' performance in the training context. According to this

> Specific, Measurable, Agreed upon, Realistic, and Timely (SMART) goals enhance learners' motivation and performance during training.

long history of research, maximally motivating goals (i.e., the goals that lead to high-level performance) are: (1) specific, (2) measurable, (3) agreed upon, (4) realistic, (5) timely, and (6) challenging (Locke & Latham, 2002; Locke & Latham, 2006; Locke et al., 1981). Goals enhance performance by giving learners something to shoot for. When these goals are specific and measurable, learners know exactly where they are going and whether or not they have arrived (e.g., "We will decrease our communication errors by 30%"). Agreement (or "goal commitment") is essential because without commitment, learners may abandon or modify goals in the face of difficulty or initial failure; similarly, realistic goals are important to gaining this agreement and commitment. Overly difficult or impossible goals will either not be accepted to begin with, or will be abandoned quickly as learners realize that initial failures are primarily a function of goal difficulty. The timeliness of goals is also related to their specificity (e.g., "We will decrease our communication errors 30% by next quarter"). Aiming to accomplish something within a week, a month, or a year allows individuals to better understand and engage with the training process than simply hoping to accomplish something "eventually." By incorporating these goal-setting best practices into the training environment, trainers enable learners to engage with the content and process of team training in a way that encourages high levels of sustainable motivation.

## TIPS AND ADVICE

- Schedule time for goal-setting activities.
- Ensure trainees establish goals that are relevant to both team training and organizational objectives.
- Have trainees think about what they want to obtain by participating in team training.
- Help trainees develop both individual- and team-level goals.
  - o Document goals.
  - o Encourage team goals to be agreed upon by all team members.
  - o Present team goals in a shared space to serve as a visual reminder.
- Ensure goals are challenging, realistic, and measureable.

- Set both short- and long-term goals (i.e., goals for team training and goals for transfer of team training).
- Focus goals on mastering specific teamwork behaviors and processes rather than on achieving specific team performance metrics.
- Ensure that goals are flexible to the changing needs of the team.

Adapted from: Colquitt, LePine, & Noe, 2000; Locke & Latham, 2002; Salas, Weaver, & Shuffler, 2012; Seijts & Latham, 2005.

## Guideline 10: Encourage Trainees to Be Engaged During the Team Training[7]

Motivation, engagement, and interest are essential factors for driving the level of learners' participation in and benefit from the training process (Evans, 2008; Merrian, 2001; Zemke & Zemke, 1984). Learner motivation can be fostered through garnering organizational support, framing training in a positive light, and removing other possible roadblocks to motivation (e.g., apprehension, ambiguity), which we discuss in further detail subsequently. In addition to these motivational levers, team training affords another possible source of motivation—social dynamics. Though at times social dynamics can negatively affect team training effectiveness (see Principle 5), trainers may leverage these social dynamics to create a training environment that is more motivating and conducive to learning.

> For team training to be effective, the content and process of team training has to be relevant for the context within which learners work every day.

Because team training often includes training teams of individuals together who already know each other, any relationships and social hierarchies that may exist outside of the training environment may carry over into the training environment. If these relationships are not harmful to the end goal of team training, the trainer may leverage these to facilitate learner motivation. For example, formal and informal leaders may be trained alongside other less influential employees. Much like with organizational leadership support, if formal and informal leaders (i.e., individuals with significant social influence among other learners) are engaged and supportive of the training content and process, other learners are likely to follow suit (Cromwell & Kolb, 2004; French & Raven, 1959; Ibarra & Andrews, 1993).

Garnering the support of influential learners is important for more than just the immediate motivational benefits. Because the ultimate goal of any team training intervention is the application of learned content to the actual performance context, team training should simulate the performance context as much as possible (Salas, Wildman, & Piccolo, 2009). That is, learners may be able to perform teamwork or taskwork behaviors in a controlled training environment, but this learning may dissipate in the real job context. One way to counteract this (given that it does not contradict the primary goals of the training) is to ensure the learners that are the most influential in the job context are similarly influential in the training environment. If leaders are being co-trained with other employees but do not lead in the training environment, the problematic social interaction patterns that may have initially necessitated the team training will be more likely to persist. Conversely, if learners are comprehending and applying the content being taught in a social context very similar to the real job environment, this signals to learners the efficacy and relevance of the trained behaviors. In other words, for learning to last, the content, process, and environment of team training has to be relevant to the social context within which learners work every day.

---

## TIPS AND ADVICE

- Grab trainees' attention by highlighting the stimulating and exciting aspects of team training.
- Explain how trainees can personally and professionally benefit from participating in team training.
- Allow trainees to be involved in the decision to participate in team training (when possible).
- Encourage trainees to focus on learning rather than their performance during team training.
- Foster motivation and interest among the entire training group by engaging socially influential learners within the training group.
  o Ensure that socially influential learners are present during team training.
  o Communicate the utility and purpose of training to socially influential learners before training begins and outside of the training environment.
- Match the climate and content of team training to the needs and wants (when possible) of the training group.
- Reiterate the importance of training to performance (e.g., Why should I care? What's in it for me?).
- Provide trainees with realistic expectations of team training.
- Share the relative success of training as a way through which teamwork is improved.

Adapted from: Sitzmann & Ely, 2010; Tannenbaum et al., 1991; Salas, Tannenbaum, Kraiger, & Smith-Jentsch, 2012.

## Guideline 11: Facilitate Individuals' and Teams' Efficacy Beliefs That They Will Be Able to Successfully Complete Team Training[8]

Team training is often aimed at changing difficult, engrained interpersonal behaviors—this may seem to learners to be a daunting or impossible task. If learners are overwhelmed with the complexity and difficulty of team training, they will quickly lose motivation to engage in the training process. As discussed earlier, trainers may facilitate learners' motivation by appealing to their intrinsic desire to learn the training material or by encouraging them to set motivating goals. However, it is essential that learners also believe that the set goals and touted benefits of training are actually attainable. When learners understand the content and process of team training, and set difficult but achievable goals, they will be more motivated and engaged. As noted earlier, motivation theory suggests that these beliefs manifest in two ways—**instrumentality beliefs** and **expectancy beliefs** (Pritchard & Sanders, 1973; Vroom, 1964). For instrumentality beliefs, if team training is heralded as a way to reduce stress and increase productivity, team training should be communicated in such a way that these touted benefits seem plausible. An important part of expectancy beliefs are **efficacy beliefs** (Bandura, 1977) (sometimes called specific self-efficacy or training self-efficacy [Chiaburu & Marinova, 2005; Saks, 1994; Schwoerer et al., 2005]). This simply refers to learners' belief that they will be able to successfully engage in the training in such a way that they will receive the touted benefits of training. In this section, we focus on the importance of learners' efficacy beliefs.

An essential first step in facilitating learners' efficacy beliefs is assessing these beliefs. In some training contexts, learners may be more likely to be confident in their abilities to grasp the training materials than in others. Similarly, some training content may be more likely than others to elicit apprehension and lower efficacy beliefs. By assessing efficacy beliefs prior to (or at the beginning of) training, trainers may decide whether or not additional measures are required to attend to learners' efficacy beliefs. Independent of assessment, trainers can and should structure the team training environment and delivery process in such a way that low efficacy beliefs are not an issue. For example, by slowly ramping up the difficulty of training content and structuring this content such that later ideas build on earlier ideas—a technique known as scaffolding—learners are more likely to avoid unhelpful errors due simply to poor training design. Furthermore, learners can gradually experience efficacy-building "wins" if the training occasionally provides opportunities for relatively easier content.

### TIPS AND ADVICE

- Measure training efficacy (both individual and team) before the training begins to determine whether or not interventions to enhance efficacy are necessary.

- Implement practice opportunities where learners are able to experience some successes during team training.
- Enhance training efficacy with preparatory information (e.g., content overview, realistic previews), especially in stressful environments.
- Promote the use of scaffolding in building team training.
- Reiterate the importance of training to performance (e.g., Why should I care? What's in it for me?).
- Provide trainees with realistic expectations of team training.
- Share the relative success of training as a way through which teamwork is improved.

Adapted from: Cannon-Bowers et al., 1998; Colquitt, et al., 2000; Salas et al., 2012.

## Principle 5: Provide a Safe, Non-Critical Team Training Environment[9]

Regardless of how interested learners are in the content and benefits of team training, and despite the supportive efforts of organizational leadership, learners must also not be impeded from engaging in the learning process *in the actual training environment.* Research has

> If the training environment is characterized by apprehension or ambiguity, the learning process will be severely impeded.

suggested several factors immediate to the training environment which may hinder the learning process: (1) apprehension regarding the actions and reactions of fellow learners (Brown & Leigh, 1996; Edmondson, 1999; Kahn, 1990), (2) aversion to making errors in training (Keith & Frese, 2008), and (3) general ambiguity or uncertainty in training. Especially in the context of team training, where learners are working with other learners to engage in training, the interpersonal dynamics between learners can be especially salient. These three factors may result in learners' withdrawal from the process or a reduction in motivation and engagement. If the training environment is characterized by apprehension or ambiguity, the learning process will be severely impeded. By addressing these potential hindrances, trainers can facilitate more positive outcomes from the training experience (Kosarzycki, Salas, DeRouin, & Fiore, 2003). In the guidelines below, we highlight these three factors—explaining the psychological foundations of the problem—and provide practical solutions for addressing these in the team training context.

## Guideline 12: Articulate What Is Expected and Appropriate Behavior During Team Training[10]

Expectations for social interaction guide everyday interpersonal behavior. When these expectations are clear, typically people adapt their behaviors to the demands of the situation. Birthday parties and business meetings are both social interactions, but they have starkly different expectations for appropriate behavior. Under normal circumstances, these expectations have a strong influence on the range of behaviors people feel comfortable engaging in. Unclear expectations or unusual social situations may induce uncertainty and apprehension as individuals attempt to ascertain what constitutes appropriate behavior. This is true in the team training context as well. If learners perceive that the training context demands civility, creativity, and participation, they will be more likely to behave as such. If they perceive no clear guidelines for interaction, then apprehension, awkwardness, and disengagement are much more likely outcomes. Furthermore, guidelines for interactions in the team training context not only direct learners towards the behaviors that are expected of them, but these expectations also enable learners to anticipate what they can expect from other learners. Unclear or unspoken expectations allow for the possibility of undesirable interactions (e.g., destructive criticism); learners' aversion to such a possibility may cause them to withdraw (i.e., psychologically and/or behaviorally) from the team training task. Individuals' sense that there may be risks associated with engaging in certain interpersonal behaviors is known as **psychological safety** (Brown & Leigh, 1996; Edmondson, 1999). In a psychologically safe team training setting, learners trust that their suggestions will not be ridiculed, their errors will not be punished, and that their interpersonal interactions will generally be pleasant. Trainers can facilitate such an environment by (1) clearly communicating and enforcing the rules and expectations for civil interpersonal interactions and (2) supporting and positively reinforcing self-expression and effort in the training environment (Brown & Leigh, 1996; Kahn, 1990).

### TIPS AND ADVICE

- Demonstrate, model, and guide desirable team training behaviors.
- Work towards establishing these norms (i.e., expectations about appropriate behavior) from the very beginning of team training.
- Consider learners' input when creating norms.
- Encourage (and reinforce) learners to make verbal gestures of support to one another.
- Avoid two major interpersonal problems frequently encountered in team training: insensitivity and unfriendliness.

- Clearly define and emphasize the need for constructive (as opposed to destructive) criticism. Provide examples of each.
- Ensure that norms cover what, when, and how team members should communicate.
- Encourage learners to identify interpersonal behaviors that might hinder the achievement of team training goals.
- Encourage learners to contribute to team training success regardless of organizational status.
- Encourage learners to ask for clarification whenever necessary.

Adapted from: Aguinis & Kraiger, 2009; Goldstein & Ford, 2002; Noe, 2002; Salas et al., 2012; Tannenbaum & Yukl, 1992.

## Guideline 13: Frame Errors Positively During Team Training[11]

Training should ideally provide learners with a safe environment (Brown & Leigh, 1996; Edmondson, 1999; Kahn, 1990) in which to make and learn from relevant mistakes. That is, learners should know that it is expected, acceptable, and potentially even desirable to make mistakes during training. One aspect of creating a training climate conducive to learning is to effectively communicate this to learners (Kahn, 1990). Allowing learners to make mistakes throughout training better simulates the job context, where there is not always a trainer to provide a safe context and guiding hand (see Pillar 3 for guidance to help match team training design with the job context). However, learners typically do not like to make errors, even in training (Keith & Frese, 2008), especially when they are being monitored. As was discussed in Guideline 12, clearly communicated expectations guide individuals' behaviors. Learners who understand that (1) errors made during training will not elicit destructive criticism or punishment, and (2) these errors are actually an important part of the teamwork training process, will experience a significant reduction in the apprehension associated with the idea of making errors (Bell & Kozlowski, 2008; Keith & Frese, 2008).

There are several ways to set expectations regarding the usefulness of errors made in training. One way to accomplish this is to inform learners that the training has been designed in such a way that trained KSAs will be addressed and re-addressed when errors are made. When learners realize they will have plenty of time and multiple chances to practice the trained KSAs, errors are less final and therefore less aversive. Additionally, by simply communicating to learners that errors are essential to the learning process, learners feel more comfortable making errors during training and are more likely to engage and participate in training.

## TIPS AND ADVICE

- Encourage learners to explore (e.g., reflect, brainstorm) and learn from mistakes when they occur.
- Communicate that it is a valuable team skill to not only be able to identify and effectively communicate errors, but that it is essential to graciously receive feedback and criticism from others.
- Inform learners that they will have multiple opportunities to practice team behaviors, so errors are not bad.
- Encourage learners to discuss both positive and negative aspects of their training progress and performance.
- Ensure adequate time and opportunities for learners to practice, as this makes errors seem less aversive and increases learners' self-efficacy.

Adapted from: Bell & Kozlowski, 2008; Keith & Frese, 2008; Salas & Cannon-Bowers, 2000a.

### Guideline 14: Reduce Any Ambiguity Surrounding Team Training[12]

A final aspect of creating an environment conducive to team training involves reducing any additional apprehension and ambiguity learners may have regarding the training process. In Guidelines 12 and 13, we discussed the apprehension that may be associated with undesirable interpersonal interactions as well as learners' aversion to making errors in training. Another component of a "safe" training environment that is conducive to learning is the reduction of ambiguity. **Ambiguity** in the training context refers to learners' sense that things are unclear and/or unpredictable. Ambiguity brings with it a sense of apprehension. As we discussed in Guideline 12, trainers can reduce learners' apprehension of possible negative interactions in the training environment by clearly communicating the social expectations during team training, thereby reducing ambiguity (Brown & Leigh, 1996; Kahn, 1990). Beyond ambiguity and apprehension related to interpersonal relations and training difficulty, learners may be unclear about other things as well. For example, learners may wonder what the purpose of team training is (Salas, Rosen, & King, 2009), whether the training will run too long and impinge upon their other responsibilities (Burke et al., 2007), or they may just generally wonder what is going to happen next (Salas, Burke, & Cannon-Bowers, 2002; Salas, Rosen, & King, 2009). These may induce apprehension to be sure, but they may also simply distract learners' attention, as they wonder and think about all these irrelevant things. In order to learn, learners have to take in and think about all the *relevant* information provided during team training. However, logistical issues such as length or order of training are certainly *not* relevant to improving learners' teamwork skills—if learners are distracted from thinking about these peripheral issues, they are less likely to learn the central content of team training. Trainers can circumvent this potential issue by addressing any areas of ambiguity at the outset of training.

---

### TIPS AND ADVICE

- Communicate and respect learners' time constraints to keep the focus on team training, not scheduling.
- Communicate organizationally defined team training goals and objectives clearly (see Guideline 16) through advanced organizers (see also Guideline 21).
- Create a structured team training environment through sufficient preparation.
- Depict team training flow and corresponding timeline(s) clearly.

Adapted from: Salas et al., 2002; Salas & Cannon-Bowers, 2000a.

---

## Notes

1  Baumgartel, Reynolds, & Pathan, 1984; Broad & Newstrom, 1992; Facteau, Dobbins, Russell, Ladd, & Kudish, 1995; Kennedy, Loughry, Klammer, & Beyerlein, 2008
2  Salas & Cannon-Bowers, 2000a
3  Bunch, 2007; Kozlowski, Brown, Weissbein, Cannon-Bowers, & Salas, 2000; Salas & Cannon-Bowers, 2000b
4  Beier & Kanfer, 2010; Cannon-Bowers & Salas, 1998; Colquitt, LePine, & Noe, 2000; Klein, Sims, & Salas, 2006; Mathieu & Martineau, 1997; Salas et al., 2008; Salas & Kozlowski, 2010
5  Quiñones, 2001; Salas et al., 2009; Tannenbaum, Mathieu, Salas, & Cannon-Bowers, 1991
6  Smith-Jentsch, Cannon-Bowers, Tannenbaum, & Salas, 2008; Locke & Latham, 2002; Locke & Latham, 2006
7  Goldstein & Ford, 2002; Noe, 2002
8  Chiaburu & Marinova, 2005; Colquitt et al., 2000
9  Noe, 2002; Salas et al., 2012
10  Noe, 2002; Salas et al., 2012; Tannenbaum et al., 1991
11  Keith & Frese, 2008
12  Brown & Leigh, 1996; Burke et al., 2007; Kahn, 1990

## References

Aguinis, H., & Kraiger, K. (2009). Benefits of training and development for individuals and teams, organizations, and society. *Annual Review of Psychology, 60*, 451–474.

Amabile, T.M. (1996). *Creativity and innovation in organizations*. Boston, MA: Harvard Business School.

Axtell, C.M., Maitlis, S., & Yearta, S.K. (1997). Predicting immediate and longer term transfer of training. *Personnel Review, 26*(3), 201–213.

Bandura, A. (1977). Self-efficacy: Toward a unifying theory of behavioral change. *Psychological Review, 84*(2), 191–215.

Baumgartel, H.J., Reynolds, M.J.I., & Pathan, R.Z. (1984). How personality and organizational climate variables moderate the effectiveness of management development programmes: A review and some recent research findings. *Management and Labour Studies, 9*(1), 1–16.

Beier, M.E., & Kanfer, R. (2010). Motivation in training and development: A phase perspective. In E. Salas & S.W.J. Kozlowski (Eds.), *Learning, training, and development in organizations* (p. 65–98). New York, NY: Taylor & Francis Group.

Bell, B. S., & Kozlowski, S.W.J. (2008). Active learning: Effects of core training design elements on self-regulatory processes, learning, and adaptability. *Journal of Applied Psychology, 93*(2), 296–316.

Bierly III, P. E., Kessler, E. H., & Christensen, E. W. (2000). Organizational learning, knowledge and wisdom. *Journal of Organizational Change Management, 13*(6), 595–618.

Broad, M. L., & Newstrom, J. W. (1992). *Transfer of training: Action-packed strategies to ensure high payoff from training investments.* Boston, MA: Da Capo Press.

Brown, S. P., & Leigh, T. W. (1996). A new look at psychological climate and its relationship to job involvement, effort, and performance. *Journal of Applied Psychology, 81*(4), 358–368.

Bunch, K. J. (2007). Training failure as a consequence of organizational culture. *Human Resource Development Review, 6*(2), 142–163.

Burke, C. S., Hess, K., Salas, E., Priest, H., Paley, M., & Riedel, S. (2007). Preparing for operations in complex environments: The leadership of multicultural teams. In R. Hoffman (Ed.), *Expertise out of context: Proceedings of the sixth international conference on naturalistic decision making* (pp. 403–427). London, UK: Psychology Press.

Burke, L. A., & Hutchins, H. M. (2007). Training transfer: An integrative literature review. *Human Resource Development Review, 6*, 263–296.

Cannon-Bowers, J. A., Rhodenizer, L., Salas, E., & Bowers, C. A. (1998). A framework for understanding pre-practice conditions and their impact on learning. *Personnel Psychology, 51*(2), 291–320.

Cannon-Bowers, J. A., & Salas, E. (1998). Current directions in psychological science. Team performance and training in complex environments: Recent findings from applied research. *Current Directions in Psychological Science, 7*(3), 83–87.

Chiaburu, D. S., & Marinova, S. V. (2005). What predicts skills transfer? An exploratory study of goal orientation, training self-efficacy and organizational supports. *International Journal of Training & Development, 9*(2), 110–123.

Colquitt, J. A., LePine, J. A., & Noe, R. A. (2000). Toward an integrative theory of training motivation: A meta-analytic path analysis of 20 years of research. *Journal of Applied Psychology, 85*(5), 678–707.

Cromwell, S. E., & Kolb, J. A. (2004). An examination of work-environment support factors affecting transfer of supervisory skills training to the workplace. *Human Resource Development Quarterly, 15*(4), 449–471.

Edmondson, A. (1999). Psychological safety and learning behavior in work teams. *Administrative Science Quarterly, 44*, 350–383.

Egan, T. M., Yang, B., & Bartlett, K. R. (2004). The effects of organizational learning culture and job satisfaction on motivation to transfer learning and turnover intention. *Human Resource Development Quarterly, 15*(3), 279–301.

Evans, J.S.B.T. (2008). Dual-processing accounts of reasoning, judgment, and social cognition. *Annual Review of Psychology, 59*, 255–278.

Facteau, J. D., Dobbins, G. H., Russell, J.E.A., Ladd, R. T., & Kudish, J. D. (1995). The influence of general perceptions of the transfer of training on pretraining motivation and perceived training transfer. *Journal of Management, 21*(1), 1–25.

French, J., & Raven, B. (1959). The basis of social power. In D. Cartwright (Ed.), *Studies in social power* (pp. 150–167). Ann Arbor, MI: University of Michigan.

Goldstein, I.L., & Ford, J. (2002). *Training in organizations: Needs assessment, development, and evaluation* (4th ed.). Belmont, CA: Wadsworth/Thomson Learning.

Guay, F., Vallerand, R. J., & Blanchard, C. (2000). On the assessment of situational intrinsic and extrinsic motivation: The Situational Motivation Scale (SIM). *Motivation and Emotion, 24*(3), 175–213.

Ho, V. T., Rousseau, D. M., & Levesque, L. L. (2006). Social networks and the psychological contract: Structural holes, cohesive ties, and beliefs regarding employer obligations. *Human Relations, 59*, 459–481.

Hurley, R. F., & Hult, G.T.M. (1998). Innovation, market orientation, and organizational learning: An integration and empirical examination. *The Journal of Marketing, 62*, 42–54.

Ibarra, H., & Andrews, S. B. (1993). Power, social influence, and sense making: Effects of network centrality and proximity on employee perceptions. *Administrative Science Quarterly, 38*(2), 277–303.

Isen, A. M., & Reeve, J. (2005). The influence of positive affect on intrinsic and extrinsic motivation: Facilitating enjoyment of play, responsible work behavior, and self-control. *Motivation and Emotion, 29*(4), 297–325.

Kahn, W. A. (1990). Psychological conditions of personal engagement and disengagement at work. *Academy of Management Journal, 33*(4), 692–724.

Keith, N., & Frese, M. (2008). Effectiveness of error management training: A meta-analysis. *Journal of Applied Psychology, 93*(1), 59–69.

Kennedy, F.A., Loughry, M.L., Klammer, T.P., & Beyerlein, M.M. (2008). Effects of organizational support on potency in work teams: The mediating role of team processes. *Small Group Research, 40*, 72–93.

Klein, C., Sims, D. E., & Salas, E. (2006). Training evaluation. In W. Karwowski (Ed.), *International encyclopedia of ergonomics and human factors* (pp. 2434–2439). Boca Raton, FL: CRC Press.

Kosarzycki, M. P., Salas, E., DeRouin, R., & Fiore, S. M. (2003). Distance learning in organizations: A review and assessment of future needs. In E. Salas (Series Ed.) & D. Stone (Vol. Ed.), *Advances in human performance and cognitive engineering research: Human resources technology* (Vol. 3, pp. 69–98). Boston, MA: JAI Press.

Kozlowski, S., Brown, K., Weissbein, D., Cannon-Bowers, J., & Salas, E. (2000). A multilevel approach to training effectiveness. In K.J. Klein, K. & S.W.J. Kozlowski (Eds.), *Multi level theory, research, and methods in organizations* (pp. 157–210). San Francisco, CA: Jossey-Bass.

Lim, H., Lee, S. G., & Nam, K. (2007). Validating E-learning factors affecting training effectiveness. *International Journal of Information Management, 27*(1), 22–35.

Locke, E.A., & Latham, G.P. (1990). *A theory of goal setting & task performance.* Englewood Cliffs, NJ: Prentice-Hall.

Locke, E. A., & Latham, G. P. (2002). Building a practically useful theory of goal setting and task motivation: A 35-year odyssey. *American Psychologist, 57*(9), 705–717.

Locke, E. A., & Latham, G. P. (2006). New directions in goal-setting theory. *Current Directions in Psychological Science, 15*(5), 265–268.

Locke, E.A., Shaw, K. N., Saari, L. M., & Latham, G. P. (1981). Goal setting and task performance: 1969–1980. *Psychological Bulletin, 90*(1), 125–152.

Mathieu, J. E., & Martineau, J. W. (1997). Individual and situational influences in training motivation. In J. K. Ford, S.W.J. Kozlowski, K. Kraiger, E. Salas & M. S. Teachout (Eds.), *Improving training effectiveness in work organizations* (pp. 193–222). Mahwah, NJ: Lawrence Erlbaum Associates.

Mento, A. J., Locke, E.A., & Klein, H. J. (1992). Relationship of goal level to valence and instrumentality. *Journal of Applied Psychology, 77*(4), 395–405.

Merrian, S. B. (2001). Andragogy and self-directed learning: Pillars of adult learning theory. *New Directions for Adult and Continuing Education, 89*, 3–14.

Morrell, D. L., & Korsgaard, M.A. (2011). Training in context: Toward a person-by-situation view of voluntary training. *Human Resource Development Quarterly, 22*(3), 323–342.

Noe, R.A. (2002). *Employee training and development.* (2nd ed.). Boston, MA: McGraw-Hill/Irwin.

Prince, M. (2004). Does active learning work? A review of the research. *Journal of Engineering Education, 93*(3), 223–231.

Pritchard, R. D., & Sanders, M. S. (1973). The influence of valence, instrumentality, and expectancy on effort and performance. *Journal of Applied Psychology, 57*(1), 55–60.

Quiñones, M.A. (2001). Contextual influence on training effectiveness. In M.A. Quiñones & A. Ehrenstein (Eds.), *Training for a rapidly changing workplace* (pp. 177–200). Washington, DC: APA Books.

Saks, A. M. (1994). Moderating effects of self-efficacy for the relationship between training method and anxiety and stress reactions of newcomers. *Journal of Organizational Behavior, 15*(7), 639–654.

Salas, E., Almeida, S.A., Salisbury, M., King, H., Lazzara, E. H., Lyons, R., . . . McQuillan, R. (2009). What are the critical success factors for team training in health care? *Journal on Quality and Patient Safety, 35*(8), 398–405.

Salas, E., Burke, C.S., & Cannon-Bowers, J.A. (2002). What we know about designing and delivering team training: Tips and guidelines. In K. Kraiger (Ed.), *Creating, implementing, and managing effective training and development: State-of-the-art lessons for practice* (pp. 234–259). San Francisco, CA: Jossey-Bass.

Salas, E., & Cannon-Bowers, J. A. (2000a). Designing training systems systematically. In E. A. Locke (Ed.), *The Blackwell handbook of principles of organizational behavior* (pp. 43–59). Malden, MA: Blackwell Publisher.

Salas, E., & Cannon-Bowers, J.A. (2000b). The anatomy of team training. In S. Tobias & J.D. Fletcher (Eds.), *Training & retraining: A handbook for business, industry, government, and the military* (pp. 312–335). New York, NY; Macmillan Reference USA.

Salas, E., & Kozlowski, S.W.J. (2010). Learning, training, and development in organizations: Much progress and a peak over the horizon. In E. Salas & S. Kozlowski (Eds.), *Learning, training, and development in organizations* (pp. 461–476). New York, NY: Routledge.

Salas, E., Rosen, M. A., & King, H. B. (2009). Integrating teamwork into the "DNA" of graduate medical education: Principles for simulation-based training. *Journal of Graduate Medical Education, 1*(2), 243–244.

Salas, E., Tannenbaum, S.I., Kraiger, K., & Smith-Jentsch, K.A. (2012). The science of training and development in organizations: What matters in practice. *Psychological Science in the Public Interest, 13*(2), 74–101.

Salas, E., Weaver, S.J., & Shuffler, M.L. (2012). Learning, training, and development in organizations. In S.J. Kozlowski (Ed.), *The Oxford handbook of organizational psychology, Vol. 1* (pp. 330–372). New York, NY: Oxford University Press.

Salas, E., Wildman, J. L., & Piccolo, R. F. (2009). Using simulation-based training to enhance management education. *Academy of Management Learning & Education, 8*(4), 559–573.

Salas, E., Wilson, K. A., Lazzara E. H., King, H. B., Augenstein, J. S., Robinson, D. W., & Birnbach, D. J. (2008). Simulation-based training for patient safety: 10 principles that matter. *Journal of Patient Safety, 4*(1), 3–8.

Schwoerer, C. E., May, D. R., Hollensbe, E. C., & Mencl, J. (2005). General and specific self-efficacy in the context of a training intervention to enhance performance expectancy. *Human Resource Development Quarterly, 16*(1), 111–129.

Seijts, G. H., & Latham, G. P. (2005), Learning versus performance goals: When should each be used? *The Academy of Management Executive, 19*(1), 124–131.

Sims, D. E., Salas, E., & Burke, C. S. (2005). Promoting effective team performance through training. In S. Wheelan (Ed.), *The handbook of group research and practice* (pp. 407–425). Thousand Oaks, CA: Sage Publications.

Sitzmann, T., & Ely, K. (2010). Sometimes you need a reminder: The effects of prompting self-regulation on regulatory processes, learning, and attrition. *Journal of Applied Psychology, 93*(1), 132–144.

Smith-Jentsch, K. A., Cannon-Bowers, J. A., Tannenbaum, S. I., & Salas, E. (2008). Guided team self-correction: Impacts on team mental models, processes, and effectiveness. *Small Group Research, 39*(3), 303–327.

Tannenbaum, S. I., Mathieu, J. E., Salas, E., & Cannon-Bowers, J. A. (1991). Meeting trainees' expectations: The influence of training fulfillment on the development of commitment, self-efficacy, and motivation. *Journal of Applied Psychology, 76*(6), 759–769.

Tannenbaum, S. I., & Yukl, G. (1992). Training and development in work organizations. *Annual Review of Psychology, 43*, 399–441.

Tharenou, P. (2001). The relationship of training motivation to participation in training and development. *Journal of Occupational and Organizational Psychology, 74*(5), 599–621.

Vroom, V. H. (1964). *Work and motivation.* New York, NY: Wiley.

Zemke, R., & Zemke, S. (1984). 30 things we know for sure about adult learning. *Innovation Abstracts, 6*(8).

# 4

# PILLAR 3

## Design Team Training for Maximum Accessibility, Usability, and Learnability

Designing the training program without first understanding the organization and its specific training requirements will likely undermine the effectiveness and ultimate utility of team training.

**How should team training content be developed and delivered to learners?** By the time one begins to design team training, training needs should have already been identified through an analytical process to understand the organization, its people, the level of its workforce's talent, and its teams' strengths and weaknesses (see Chapter 2). Team training content and materials will be highly influenced by the findings from early needs analysis, which will serve as the starting line and roadmap for the resulting training (Salas & Stagl, 2009). Once training needs and requirements are identified, the development of instructional content and materials can take place. We cannot stress enough that designing a training program without first understanding the organization and its specific team training needs, requirements, and conditions will undermine the effectiveness and ultimate utility of team training.

Team training design involves thoughtful planning and generation of course content. During the team training design process, the training developer focuses on delineating learning objectives, outlining course content to meet stated objectives, and selecting appropriate instructional strategies and learning technologies given what is known about the organization, the nature of the learners, and their work (Salas, Tannenbaum, Kraiger, & Smith-Jentsch, 2012). This process should be conducted in a manner that will maximize training accessibility, usability, and learnability. By **accessibility**, we mean that team training should be made available to all learners requiring instruction. It should not be difficult for learners to attend and engage in training, which would discourage participation. Training should also be designed to promote **usability**, that is, the easy implementation and facilitation of a finalized training program. If the individuals responsible for delivering training are unduly challenged or confused by the implementation process, training is unlikely to be conducted efficiently or effectively. Last, training design should promote maximum **learnability**; training should be designed in such a way that by participating in training, learners are able to improve the KSAs targeted by training and be capable of performing them at the highest level possible.

While designing training for maximum accessibility, usability, and learnability does require an intimate knowledge of the organization, the learners, and their work, it also necessitates an understanding of training as more than just a one-time event. Training should be thought of as a closed-loop system composed of multiple steps and components with the aim of imparting the KSAs necessary to improve performance in another environment (Goldstein & Ford, 2002). Broadly, this system may be thought of as involving preparation and planning, delivery, and evaluation of training programs (Gregory, Feitosa, Driskell, Salas, & Vessey, 2013; Salas & Stagl, 2009). Designing team training falls under the category of preparation and planning and consists of evidence-based activities whose products build on each other to create training that is strongly connected to training needs. Each of these activities and system components are described below, along with practical guidelines and advice for executing them.

Under this pillar we present four principles and 17 guidelines to assist team training designers with the details of planning and creating team training content. The four principles prompt training developers and instructional designers to systematically design team training (Principle 6); leverage information, demonstration, practice, and feedback within team training designs (Principle 7); employ team training delivery strategies, tools, and technology appropriate for meeting the needs of the organization, team, and trainees (Principle 8); and ensure instructors are prepared to teach (Principle 9). We elaborate on each of these and their respective guidelines below.

## Principle 6: Systematically Design Team Training Based on What's Scientifically Shown to Be Effective[1]

Once team training needs are known, training designers may begin systematically creating team training. "Systematic" simply means that training is intentionally designed to meet a specific need by following a predetermined, evidence-based process; this process consists of formulating learning objectives, facilitating controlled learning experiences, establishing performance criteria, conducting performance assessment, and providing helpful feedback (Goldstein & Ford, 2002). This step-by-step process begins with the specification of learning objectives (see Guideline 16), which are further elaborated into specific, trainable KSAs that are appropriate for the learning context (Guideline 17). After identifying learning objectives and targeted KSAs, the training developer identifies appropriate training strategies (Guideline 18) and organizes material in a meaningful way (Guideline 19). When an initial version of the training program has been developed, it must be pilot tested (Guideline 20). By following this evidence-based process, designers will be better able to create a team training program that deftly meets the identified need(s) and suits the organizational context. This will render programs that are effective and useful within the organization. Furthermore, forming partnerships between subject matter experts (SMEs) and learning experts will improve, though not necessarily make easier, the training design process (Salas, Wilson, Burke, & Priest, 2005). We present and elaborate on each of the following guidelines below.

> Subject matter experts contribute domain-specific knowledge whereas learning experts can guide training development.

## Guideline 15: Form Partnerships Between Subject Matter Experts and Learning Experts[2]

Establishing partnerships between learning experts and subject matter experts (SMEs) will provide a helpful dynamic when designing and delivering training (Salas et al., 2005). SMEs are an invaluable source of task domain knowledge and can easily articulate task-related needs and requirements (Salas, Cannon-Bowers, Rhodenizer, & Bowers, 1999; Salas et al., 2005). However, SMEs do not necessarily have the knowledge and skills needed to create a rigorous instructional program and positive learning environment (Salas et al., 2005). Learning experts, on the other hand, can guide evidence-based design to ensure that training requirements (i.e., competencies and learning objectives) are identified and that instructional components build from them. This can be accomplished through the use of evidence-based techniques—such as structured and semi-structured interviews and focus groups—to get at a SME's underlying task knowledge (see Appendix 2 for example interview questions). Briefly, structured interviews ask the same question of every person being interviewed. Conversely, semi-structured interviews follow a predetermined format, but afford some flexibility to allow the interviewer and respondent to explore certain issues in greater (or less) detail.

SMEs can contribute to identifying performance contexts that are relevant to the trainees, and help ensure that training material is organized so that it is easily understood by trainees. Executing training design without one or the other expert input would increase the probability of creating an ineffective training program which fails to meet the training needs. When designing team training, mutual partnerships between SMEs and learning experts are a must.

In order to cultivate these partnerships, instructional designers and training developers should encourage SMEs from the organization to participate in the development of team training content. It may help to explain the importance of team training to SMEs and describe how their input would be instrumental in ensuring the resulting product is useful. Additionally, describing the benefits SMEs can derive from their involvement may encourage voluntary participation: SMEs may include potential learners. In fact, some research shows that including learners in the design process (Tharenou, 2001) positively relates to their motivation to engage in training. Offering involvement in training design may not only help to make the team training more effective, but may also serve to prime potential learners to accept the benefits of training. It should be noted, however, that there can be pitfalls in including possible learners or other SMEs in training-related decisions (Baldwin, Magjuka, & Loher, 1991; Mathieu, Tannenbaum, & Salas, 1992). Instructional designers and training developers should only seek input from learners or other SMEs when they plan to actively incorporate these contributions. Obtaining feedback without utilizing it may send a message to learners that their feedback is not valued, which can harm learner motivation (Quiñones, 1995; Quiñones, 1997).

The benefits of partnering SMEs and learning experts are best realized when frequent and effective interaction and collaboration are facilitated. One way to accomplish this is to create a training design team (comprised of SMEs and learning experts) with regularly scheduled project meetings. During the first team meeting, team member roles should be clearly identified; additionally, the importance of their collaboration and contribution should be reiterated. Subsequent meetings should follow the training design process outlined below (e.g., specification of learning objectives, context, KSAs, etc.).

## TIPS AND ADVICE

- Invite subject matter experts (SMEs) in the organization to participate in team training development.
  - o Explain the importance of involving SMEs in team training development and articulate the benefit SMEs can derive by participating in training development.
- Schedule team meetings between SMEs and learning experts.
  - o Clearly identify the roles of each SME and learning expert and explain why the collaboration is important.
- Leverage learning experts' knowledge of training and teamwork science to ensure training design activities follow the prescribed process.
- Rely on SMEs to inform the development of team training content, the preferred examples and practice context, and to provide insider information about the future trainees.

> o Use scientifically-grounded techniques (e.g., structured and semi-structured interviews) to get at SME's underlying knowledge that must be reflected in team training content.
>
> Adapted from: Aguinis & Kraiger, 2009; Kraiger, McLinden, & Casper, 2004.

## Guideline 16: Define Learning Objectives to Be Targeted During Team Training in Advance[3]

> Learning objectives are action-oriented, specific, and measurable statements that describe what learners are expected to know, be able to do, and/or feel as a result of attending training.

Learning objectives are action-oriented, specific, and measureable statements describing what learners are expected to know, be able to do, and/or feel as a result of attending training (Rosen, Salas, Silvestri, Wu, & Lazzara, 2008; Salas et al., 2012). Action-oriented learning objectives begin with a verb and denote that learners will be able to think, do, or feel something. Specific learning objectives refer to the level of detail with which objectives describe the knowledge, skill, or attitude to be learned. Learning objectives should be specific enough to be observable so that assessors can identify when learners have obtained the objective. Last, learning objectives need to be measurable. Because measurement facilitates feedback learning (Boud & Falchikov, 2006), it is essential for accelerating expertise as it lays the foundation on which learners know what aspects of performance to maintain or adjust (Salas, Rosen, Weaver, Held, & Weissmuller, 2010).

Information collected during TTNA forms the basis for crafting the learning objectives that frame team training. This information enables team training developers to align learning objectives with organizational goals and outcomes and tailor learning objectives to the learners' current ability level. Part of this alignment is deciding whether team training will be developed to target context-driven, team-contingent, task-contingent, or transportable teamwork competencies. **Transportable teamwork** competencies have the widest range of applicability, and many team training programs have been created with the aim of training a specific set of such competencies (e.g., ability to resolve conflict). As the name suggests, learners can generalize transportable competencies to any team and any team task with which they become involved. The other competency types are much narrower in focus. For instance, **task-contingent** refers to those competencies that are only applicable to certain team tasks (e.g., knowledge of procedures for completing the task), whereas **team-contingent** competencies refer to those of which a particular team is in need (e.g., knowledge of teammate

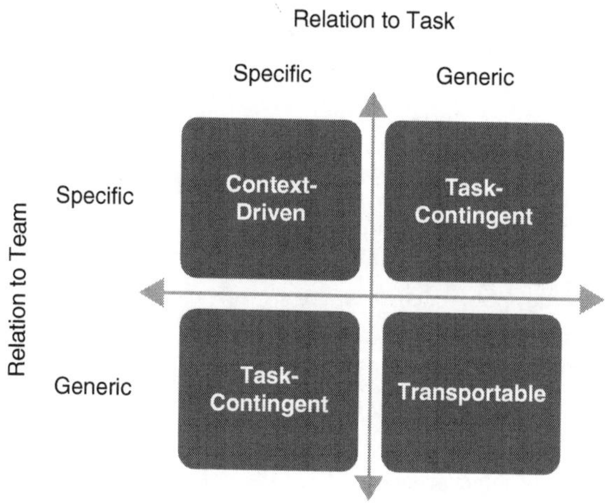

Relation to Task

Specific        Generic

Relation to Team

Specific

Generic

Context-Driven

Task-Contingent

Task-Contingent

Transportable

**FIGURE 4.1.** Types of Team Competencies.
Adapted from Cannon-Bowers et al., 1995.

characteristics). **Context-driven** competencies are the most narrow as they refer to competencies that a particular team must have in order to perform a particular task at some minimally accepted level (e.g., collective efficacy) (Cannon-Bowers, Tannenbaum, Salas, & Volpe, 1995). Figure 4.1 presents these general categories of team competencies and suggests that the team and task characteristics will determine the type of competencies team training requires.

As discussed earlier, ideal learning objectives are action-oriented, specific, and measurable. Vague learning objectives simply specify the end state that learners should attain after training, whereas more precise objectives clearly specify the demonstrable knowledge, behavioral, and/or attitudinal changes that indicate that training has met the broadly stated objectives (see Guideline 17 for more discussion of specific and context-driven KSAs). Finally, learning objectives must fully, explicitly, and strictly describe what learners must learn from training—learning objectives should not be muddied by discussing objectives or outcomes superfluous to the training needs. Team training should only include learning objectives that are essential to fostering teamwork KSAs needed to complete team tasks in the organization.

## TIPS AND ADVICE

- Use information collected during the team training needs analysis to inform the development of team training learning objectives in order to ensure learning objectives meet team training needs (see Principle 1).

- Align team training learning objectives with organizational goals and out-comes.
- Consider learners' current ability level when developing learning objectives.
- Determine whether team training should target context-driven, team-contingent, task-contingent, or transportable teamwork competen-cies in order to meet the learning objectives.
- Establish learning objectives that are specific and measureable.
- Explicate general and specific team training objectives—general objec-tives specify the end state the trainees should attain whereas specific objectives (i.e., KSAs) identify behaviors that must be performed to meet the general objectives.
- Only include learning objectives that are essential for fostering the devel-opment of teamwork KSAs needed to complete team tasks; avoid includ-ing irrelevant learning objectives.
  o  Emphasize teamwork KSAs over taskwork KSAs in team training.

Adapted from: Cannon-Bowers et al., 1995; Noe, 2002; Salas & Cannon-Bowers, 2000b; Surface, 2012.

## Guideline 17: Select the Specific Teamwork Knowledge, Skills, and/or Attitudes to Be Targeted in Team Training[4]

KSAs represent what learners must know (i.e., knowledge), be able to do (i.e., skills), and/or feel (i.e., attitudes) in order to demonstrate proficiency on the learning objectives (see Chapter 1 and Appendix 1). For instance, a learning objective may call for learners to "demonstrate knowledge of other team members' roles." The manifestation of KSAs indicating such proficiency may be that the learner requests assistance from appropriate supporting roles during a simulation. Also, like learning objectives, KSAs will be defined based on the outcome of prior investigation of team training needs. However, KSAs are more granular than learning objectives—multiple KSAs may be needed to demonstrate proficiency on a single learning objective—and are often expressly linked back to job tasks (Goldstein & Ford, 2002). This can make them more context-specific than learning objectives because KSAs describe the specific proficiencies needed to effectively perform team tasks. In the case of team training, these tasks will involve the interdependent actions of individuals working towards a common goal and the KSAs targeted by train-ing will represent a nuanced manifestation of teamwork competencies (e.g., synchronizing actions) rather than task-specific capabilities (e.g., word processing skills).

Because KSAs can be thought of as representing learning objectives in a more granular and context-specific

> Measurement is paramount to learning—pay attention to the learning process. It is how we know that learning has occurred.

level, they should be clearly linked to previously defined team training learning objectives (Rosen et al., 2008). Known KSA deficiencies, especially those that have caused errors during team tasks, should be of primary concern in team training. These should, of course, be diagnosed prior to beginning team training design (see Pillar 1 for more detail regarding the needs diagnosis process). The purpose of team training is to facilitate adaptive team behaviors (Burke, Salas, Wilson-Donnelly, & Priest, 2004), including, but not limited to, competencies such as situation awareness, communication, leadership, adaptability, and compensatory behavior (Salas, Burke, & Cannon-Bowers, 2002; Salas, Sims, Klein, & Burke, 2003). Last, the selected KSAs must be measurable and the appropriate measurement techniques should be identified (see Principle 10 for more information). One important point here is that, although we do not discuss measurement *specifics* until Pillar 4, measurement *planning* is also an important step within the training design process. We highly encourage readers to read about the specifics of measurement and training evaluation under Pillar 4 before engaging in any training design initiatives.

## TIPS AND ADVICE

- Link targeted KSAs to previously defined team training learning objectives.
- Seek to diagnose KSA deficiencies that occurred during team tasks that led to errors (see Principle 1).
- Consider KSAs that facilitate adaptive team behaviors such as situation awareness, communication, team leadership, adaptability, and compensatory behavior.
- Ensure KSAs targeted in team training are task relevant and can be used on the job.
- Ensure teamwork KSAs can be measured and identify appropriate measurement techniques (see also Principle 10).

Adapted from: Cannon-Bowers et al., 1995; Noe, 2002; Rosen et al., 2008; Salas, Oser, Cannon-Bowers, & Daskarolis-Kring, 2002.

## Guideline 18: Select Instructional Strategies That Foster the Development of Teamwork Competencies[5]

**Well-Designed Training**

1. Clearly communicates the training purpose and objectives
2. Centers on content meaningful to learners
3. Includes learning aids
4. Incorporates practice opportunities
5. Provides feedback
6. Demonstrates key points
7. Is coordinated effectively

Salas and colleagues define instructional strategies as the "tools, methods, and context that are combined and integrated to create a training delivery approach" (Salas et al., 2012, p. 85). As we have previously discussed, how team training is designed—that is, how training is planned, organized, and structured—greatly impacts its ultimate utility and effectiveness. Fortunately, there is an evidence base that guides selection of instructional strategies. For example, Noe and Colquitt (2002) reviewed the training literature and identified a number of characteristics of well-designed training that facilitate the learning and transfer of KSAs to the performance environment. They found training is maximally effective when: (a) learners understand the training purpose, learning objectives, and expected outcomes; (b) training content is meaningful to learners and the examples, exercises, and assignments are relevant to the job and team; (c) learning aids are provided to help learners assimilate, organize, and recall training content; (d) learners are given the opportunity to practice their newfound KSAs in a physically and psychologically safe environment that allows them to make and learn from errors; (e) learners are provided subsequent feedback on learning and performance from instructor(s), peers, or even the task itself; (f) learners are able to observe and interact with other learners during training; and (g) the training program is effectively coordinated. Training developers should take great care to include most, and ideally all, of these characteristics in their own training programs (Salas, DeRouin, & Littrell, 2005).

In the delivery of training, a thorough strategy accomplishes four things (Salas & Cannon-Bowers, 2001). First, it imparts the necessary information learners need in order to be able to perform at a minimally acceptable level. In the case of team training, this information will center on instruction regarding non-technical (i.e., interpersonal or teamwork) information. Second, it demonstrates the desired behavior, cognitions, or attitudes expected. Third, it provides opportunities for learners to practice teamwork KSAs. Fourth, it gives learners feedback on how they are doing in regards to their learning and practice performance and, therefore, allows for the affirmation of correct behaviors and remediation of incorrect or undesired behavior. Because these four strategy components are so critical to effective team training programs they are each addressed in significantly more detail in Guidelines 21–24 under Principle 7. In order to achieve the varied strengths while avoiding the weaknesses of different instructional strategies, training developers should leverage multiple instructional strategies in each training program.

---

## TIPS AND ADVICE

- Adopt multiple instructional strategies to leverage the strength of varied strategies together (e.g., practice and feedback).
- Choose strategies that best align with unique team needs. For example, if team training centers on novel competencies, multiple demonstrations may be beneficial; alternatively, remedial training of previously learned competencies may be more practice and feedback focused.
- Consider the pros and cons associated with each strategy in light of team training objectives and contextual constraints.

Adapted from: Salas & Cannon-Bowers, 2000b.

---

### Guideline 19: Organize Team Training Material in a Manner That Will Facilitate Learning[6]

The organization of team training content is also important to consider during training design. How content is organized and presented can strongly influence how much learning occurs during team training. For instance, information can be presented in a manner that facilitates learning by clearly demonstrating the connections between training concepts (Sweller, van Merriënboer, & Paas, 1998). Conversely, if training materials are organized in such a way that learners struggle to see the interrelationships between concepts, learners may be unduly taxed (Cierniak, Scheiter, & Gerjects, 2008; Kirschner, 2002; Sweller et al., 1998). As a result, learning becomes stunted as learners are unable to absorb the training information efficiently. In order to avoid overtaxing learners, team training material should be designed in a straightforward manner to facilitate ease of understanding (Priest et al., 2004). This will require training developers to consider the training audience. For example, learners with more advanced declarative and procedural knowledge of the material will be less taxed by complex information and will be better able to learn from training. Conversely, novices may require a gradual training approach. Streamlining material so that requisite information is presented before more complex concepts will help learners assimilate information (Sims, Burke, Metcalf, & Salas, 2008).

---

### TIPS AND ADVICE

- Design team training material so it is easily understood by the learner—don't ignore the user!
  - o Consider the current ability level of the training audience (e.g., expert trainees may benefit from more complex or in-depth training than novices).
- Align learning modules with each other so material is streamlined.
  - o Organize material in a way that links critical concepts and ensures trainees have developed the requisite KSAs needed to learn more advanced material.

Adapted from: Gregory et al., 2013; Sims et al., 2008.

---

## Guideline 20: Pilot Test Team Training Prior to Implementation[7]

> Implementing team training without piloting risks the possibility of problems occurring that cannot be fixed without disrupting the learning process.

Remember: practice makes perfect! Even when it comes to team training it is best to pilot the program before it is rolled out in earnest. A **pilot test** is essentially a practice run of the team training program with the intent to see how well the training works in practice. Information obtained from pilot testing will allow designers to make any last-minute changes that will enhance the efficiency and effectiveness of the final product. Implementing team training without a pilot test is risky as there is no opportunity to fix any kinks (e.g., novice instructors, weak demonstrations) without potentially disrupting the learning process. For example, pilot testing provides an opportunity for training developers to confirm that the team training program emphasizes and requires learners to exhibit the targeted KSAs and to verify that any training exercises proceed as expected.

Both SMEs and learning experts should be on hand to observe team training pilot testing as these individuals will be able to employ their unique perspectives and expertise to assess the training program. To conduct a successful pilot test of team training, team training exercises should be tested with a sufficient number of participants who are comparable to the learners for whom the materials were designed. It should go without saying that any flaws in the team training program identified during pilot testing should be corrected prior to the official roll-out of the finalized training program. This may seem very obvious as the purpose of piloting training is to identify weaknesses, but it should be stated given its criticality to the success of the final product.

**TIPS AND ADVICE**

- Ensure learning experts and subject matter experts are present during pilot testing.
- Test team training exercises with a sufficient number of participants who are comparable to the learners for which the scenarios were designed.
- Confirm the team training program emphasizes and requires learners to exhibit desired KSAs.
- Verify team training exercises proceed as expected and identify factors that may influence the successful implementation of team training.
- Make sure team training instructors are prepared to facilitate the implementation of team training.
- Correct any flaws identified during pilot testing before implementing team training.

Adapted from: Beard, Salas, & Prince, 1995.

## Principle 7: Leverage Information Presentation, Demonstration, Practice, and Feedback[8]

Over 30 years of research indicates that the incorporation of information, demonstration, practice, and feedback greatly improves the utility of training programs (Salas & Cannon-Bowers, 2001). **Information** refers to the concepts and facts trainees need to learn (Salas et al., 2012). **Demonstration** provides trainees with visual representations of what information looks like in action. **Practice** affords trainees with the opportunities to apply learned KSAs in a safe and non-threatening environment. **Feedback** provides the trainee with corrective and reinforcing information regarding their performance. By leveraging the strengths of these four instructional strategies together, trainees will be more likely to learn from the training program and will be better prepared to use their new-found teamwork KSAs in the job performance setting (a phenomenon referred to as **transfer of training**) (Prince & Salas, 1999).

Despite our knowledge that practice and feedback are critical determinants of learning (Smith-Jentsch, Jentsch, Payne, & Salas, 1996), most training programs utilized in organizations tend to overemphasize information and demonstration while partially overlooking practice and feedback (Patel, 2010). This is problematic, and training developers should spend more time building practice and feedback opportunities into their team training programs. Appendix 3 presents the purpose of certain training approaches in relation to specific teamwork KSAs for reference. Similarly, Appendix 4 outlines the strengths and limitations of various team training delivery methods around the concepts presented within this principle (i.e., information, presentation, practice, and feedback).

## Guideline 21: Present Information to Trainees about the Teamwork KSAs Targeted in Team Training and Why They Are Important[9]

The presentation of information is critical to ensuring that learners have obtained the knowledge of concepts and facts needed in order to perform at a minimally accepted standard. In other words, information provides the foundation upon which learners build their understanding of teamwork. The informative aspects of team training can easily become very dry and basic, so effort should be made to make this part as engaging and motivating as possible. To start, designers should only focus on information that is likely to be novel to learners. If the group of learners to be trained is advanced in the targeted teamwork or taskwork competencies, training content should account for this and accordingly delve deeper than the basics. To orient learners to team training, training developers should build discussion of the purpose of training into the program itself. This discussion should explicate why team training is being conducted and how it is relevant to the learners. Similarly, building advanced organizers—which represent an overview of the training content and what learners can expect while engaging in training—can facilitate the presentation and delivery of information. This overview should be realistic and specify what team training will and will not accomplish. Although this content should be discussed with a sufficient level of detail so that it is actually useful (Salas et al., 2008), oversaturation of information early on in training can overwhelm learners, especially novices. Instead, information should be evenly distributed throughout the course of the training program, balanced with demonstration, practice, and feedback activities as much as possible.

---

### TIPS AND ADVICE

- Provide an overview of team training.
  - Clearly explain the purpose of team training.
  - Provide a realistic preview of what team training will and will not accomplish.
  - Make learners aware of the relationship between (1) individual development and team performance, and (2) team performance to individual preparation and accomplishment.
  - Explain the details of the team's operation, the tasks of each team member, and the KSAs required to complete the task effectively.
- Describe the critical elements of each of the teamwork KSAs addressed in training.
- Avoid presenting too much information too early and overwhelming trainees but aim to completely cover the important information trainees must know in order to learn and transfer targeted KSAs.

Adapted from: Cannon-Bowers, Rhodenizer, Salas, & Bowers, 1998.

---

## Guideline 22: Demonstrate Each Teamwork KSA[10]

Demonstration-based learning is the process of acquiring new KSAs by viewing performance exemplars (Rosen et al., 2010). The learner observes a human (either live or computer-generated) model the task or task-relevant KSAs either in real-time or through some form of prerecorded medium. By watching the model, learners are able to see first-hand the behaviors or KSAs they are expected to be able to perform (or in some cases, not perform) by the conclusion of training. Based on Albert Bandura's social learning theory, which promotes the use of observing, modeling, and vicarious reinforcement as mechanisms for modifying human performance, viewing demonstrations of targeted KSAs can improve learners' conceptual understanding of teamwork competencies and provide them with a valuable reference, which they may mimic in an attempt to improve their own performance (Bandura, 1977; Bandura, 1986; Bandura, 1991). Training developers and trainers may leverage an array of demonstration media, ranging from video, computer-generated models, or live examples by the instructor and/or participation by the learners themselves.

Demonstrations may be either positive or negative in nature. Positive demonstrations present examples of desirable teamwork competencies learners should exhibit while on the job (i.e., the performance context). Likewise, negative demonstrations present examples of harmful or counterproductive behaviors that learners should avoid while on the job. Team training programs should be designed to present both positive and negative examples of every teamwork KSA targeted by training to strengthen the opportunity to learn (Salas & Cannon-Bowers, 2001; Taylor, Russ-Eft, & Chan, 2005; Weaver, Wildman, & Salas, 2009). Demonstration is especially important in team training, as behaviors within a team context are primarily interpersonal, dynamic, and complex. Such team KSAs are difficult to properly communicate strictly via "information" (e.g., lectures, reading materials), making demonstration of team KSAs especially important. Finally, within on-the-job contexts where ideal teamwork or taskwork behaviors are ambiguous, *multiple* demonstrations of trained KSAs are especially helpful and often necessary for facilitating learning.

---

### TIPS AND ADVICE

- Use positive and negative examples to demonstrate each KSA.
- Expose learners to multiple demonstrations of the KSAs within different contexts.
- Make use of live examples, videos, and class participation.

Adapted from: Gregory et al., 2013.

## Guideline 23: Provide Learners with the Opportunity to Practice Teamwork KSAs[11]

Classical learning theory states that it is important for learners to be active during training, arguing that such activity facilitates the learning process (Astin, 1984). Cognitive theorists expand this assertion to emphasize the importance of having the learner actively produce or exhibit the KSAs to be mastered (Burke & Hutchins, 2007). This is where practice during training comes in. Well-designed training builds in opportunities for learners to practice what they have learned from the information and/or demonstration aspects of training (Noe & Colquitt, 2002; Salas & Cannon-Bowers, 2001). Practice refers to the actual application or use of the trained KSAs in a psychologically and physically safe environment where errors can be conceived of as opportunities for learning rather than potentially harmful incidents that may have grievous repercussions for customers (e.g., healthcare patients) or the employee's performance record. A physically safe environment is one in which individuals are not at risk of serious bodily harm. A psychologically safe environment is one in which individuals "feel able to show and employ one's self without fear of negative consequences to self-image, status, or career" (Khan, 1990, p. 708; see also Principle 5).

> The design of practice opportunities can significantly influence their effectiveness. Practice opportunities should be relevant, realistic, and require cognitive processes similar to those that are used on the job.

The design of practice opportunities can significantly influence their effectiveness. First and foremost, as with everything in training design, practice should be crafted to align with the training learning objectives (Salas et al., 2005). Designing multiple practice opportunities for each learning objective will maximize learning and refinement of KSA. Importantly, practice opportunities should facilitate **transfer appropriate processing**, which, simply stated, means that learners use the same cognitive processes, physical behaviors, and attitudes they would in the actual performance context (Franks, Bilbrey, Lien, & McNamara, 2000). Doing so facilitates transfer; therefore, practice opportunities should be relevant and realistic to experiences of learners outside of training (Grossman & Salas, 2011; Gregory et al., 2013; Salas et al., 2012). See the tips and advice box for more specific suggestions for how to plan such structured practice.

To help learners experience successful practice, they should be briefed on the scenario before they begin and have sufficient opportunity to work through the practice scenario on their own (Oser, Cannon-Bowers, Salas, & Dwyer, 1999; Salas, Priest, Wilson, & Burke, 2006). Practice should not be rushed and plenty of time should be dedicated to this part of training (Salas & Cannon-Bowers, 2000a). Finally, team training is most effective when intact teams train together, especially when the trained competencies are team- or context-specific (see Guideline 16 for more information about competency types). Practice sessions should be monitored so that instructors can provide developmental feedback (see Guideline 24) to learners (Salas, Burke, & Cannon-Bowers, 2002; Salas & Cannon-Bowers, 2000a; Salas, Cannon-Bowers, Smith-Jentsch, 2006).

## TIPS AND ADVICE

- Craft practice opportunities to align with team training learning objectives.
  - o Limit the number of key competencies within any given practice opportunity to avoid overly complex scenarios and promote easier measurement for feedback purposes. We recommend a maximum of five.
  - o Ensure the practice context corresponds with targeted teamwork competencies. In other words, ensure practice opportunities encourage learners to rehearse specific KSAs targeted in training.
  - o Make practice opportunities challenging yet reasonable given the team training objectives.
- Develop and apply different relevant and realistic practice opportunities.
- Ensure that team training exercises have sufficient structure so that they proceed as planned.
  - o Create a script to control for how and when scenario events unfold.
  - o Implement features into practice scenarios that require the trainee to use the same teamwork skills during training as when they are on the job.
  - o Use subject matter experts to review scenario events and scripts prior to implementing them for team training.
  - o Sequence practice opportunities according to increasing task difficulty and the degree of teamwork required.
- Brief trainees on the scenarios before they begin.
- Don't move through scenarios too quickly, afford time for trainees to respond to scenario events.
- Have intact teams practice together.
- Allow trainees to make errors and learn from mistakes during the practice scenarios (see also Guideline 13).
- Monitor practice opportunities and provide guidance when trainees deviate from the learning content (i.e., offer guided practice).

Adapted from: Gregory et al., 2013; Grossman & Salas, 2011; Rosen et al., 2008.

## Guideline 24: Provide Feedback to Trainees on Their Practice Performance[12]

**Feedback should be . . .**

1. Clear so as to avoid misinterpretation
2. Linked to a credible source
3. Frequent, but not constant
4. Targeted to specific needs of recipient

Feedback is a well-known determinant of learning, especially when paired with practice opportunities. Feedback provides needed information to learners about their performance, which can help them maximize learning. For example, Komaki and colleagues demonstrated that adding feedback to an accident prevention training program increased safety behaviors by 16% over the same accident prevention training program without feedback. Such a difference in performance is substantial, and has important consequences for accident prevention (Komaki, Heinzmann, & Lawson, 1980). Clearly, feedback meaningfully contributes to training effectiveness.

Feedback works by providing learners with a realistic understanding of their current ability level and providing precise recommendations for how performance may be improved. Learners may feel they understand a concept and are capable of appropriately applying that concept in the team context, but they may still be failing to reach their full potential or a minimally accepted standard. Feedback should not only focus on rectifying subpar performance by directing learners to focus on what they must improve (negative feedback), but it should reinforce what they are doing well (positive feedback). To support this notion, Ellis and Davidi (2005) found that when post-practice discussion dealt with both successful and unsuccessful performance, learners developed a better understanding of the environment and what constituted acceptable behavior than when feedback was only negative in nature. Ilgen, Fisher, and Taylor (1979) offer additional conclusions about providing optimal feedback:

1. Feedback must be accurately perceived by the learner to have the intended effect, yet feedback can easily be misinterpreted. This is particularly true of negative feedback.
2. Learners are sensitive to the credibility of the feedback source. Therefore, instructors wishing to employ feedback in training must appear to be experts in the training content or have earned learners' trust.
3. High-frequency or continuous feedback is not always desirable as it can interfere with learning (Schmidt & Wulf, 1997) and cause learners to feel a loss of personal control. Alternatively, continuous feedback may have the unintended effect of causing leaners to over-rely on feedback rather than forming and trusting their own performance judgments.
4. The individual learner needs to be considered when delivering feedback (Salas, Wilson, & Lyons, 2008).

In addition to these insights, several other points can guide the incorporation of feedback into team training. Performance diagnostics (i.e., measurement) during practice opportunities are essential for providing good feedback (Oser et al., 1999). The information accumulated from measurement will facilitate delivery of specific, constructive, and diagnostic feedback tailored to the individual learner and his or her needs. Moreover, this feedback should be timely. Feedback is most effective when it is delivered immediately after—but not during—practice opportunities. Feedback within team training should be focused on controllable teamwork or taskwork behaviors, rather than personal characteristics, which are not typically under the control of the learner. Feedback should also be prioritized based on the most critical issues. Approach larger issues first. For more expert learners, feedback surrounding more intricate points may be addressed. Support feedback with specific examples from the team and individual members but do not personally blame any one person for overall team success or failure. Individual-level feedback should be delivered individually to learners rather than in a group to avoid embarrassment, which would reduce learners' experience of psychological safety. Team-level feedback should, of course, be delivered to the team (Salas, Rosen, & King, 2009; Salas, Wilson, Priest, & Guthrie, 2006). Encouraging interaction and discussion during feedback sessions is helpful, so long as the discussion remains constructive. Therefore, training should promote discussion of performance, especially that surrounding development of an action plan for improving performance in the future.

## TIPS AND ADVICE

- Use information from performance diagnostics (i.e., measurement) during practice opportunities to provide feedback (see Principle 10).
- Make sure feedback is specific, constructive, timely, and prescriptive/diagnostic in order to ensure feedback fosters development of each KSA.
  o Focus on teamwork behaviors rather than personal characteristics while providing feedback.
  o Prioritize feedback based on critical performance issues.
- Organize feedback around events and learning objectives.
- Make feedback interactive and encourage input from participants.
- Reinforce good performance, correct bad performance.
- Support feedback with task- and team-relevant demonstrations and illustrations of performance during key events.
- Focus on both individual- and team-level feedback.
  o Provide feedback directly to team members in situations where the performance of one team member cannot offset the deficiencies of another.

o Provide feedback to teams with stable membership as a team.

o Provide feedback that facilitates formation of shared expectations among team members.

- Document feedback.

o Give trainees written information on the scenario events and important elements of each event.

- Engage/promote interactive discussions to create an action plan (e.g., what to do about the feedback, next steps).

Adapted from: Kluger & DeNisi, 1996; Gregory et al., 2013.

## Principle 8: Employ Team Training Delivery Strategies, Tools, and Technology Appropriate for Meeting the Needs of the Organization, Team, and Trainees[13]

After determining who would benefit from team training in the organization, assessing and/or fostering organizational support for training, and preparing a climate and setting conducive for maximum learning within the training environment, the design and delivery of the training content is the next important consideration. Important factors associated with training design and delivery also include selecting the appropriate tools and technology for providing presentations, demonstrations, and practice opportunities for learners. Additionally, instructors must be prepared to facilitate the training process. The following guidelines focus on the implementation of training technology and considerations for how the trainer can enhance the training experience for learners.

> One of the main factors that lead to individuals dropping out of training is the absence of engaging training content.

### *Guideline 25: Use Design and Delivery Methods That Are Engaging and Motivating*[14]

As described in Chapter 3, motivation is a big factor in the degree to which trainees are able to acquire and retain the learned skills from training. Obviously, motivation also refers to learners' willingness to apply learned skills to the workplace (Salas & Cannon-Bowers, 2001), leading to greater degree of transfer to the work environment (Ford, Smith, Weissbein, Gully, & Salas, 1998). Steps can be taken in the design and delivery of team training to motivate the learner to participate. One of the main factors that leads to individuals dropping out of training is the absence of engaging training content (Salas & Cannon-Bowers, 2001; Salas, DeRouin, & Littrell, 2005). Therefore, the content should not only effectively incorporate teamwork competencies, but it should be developed, delivered, and presented in ways that will actively motivate and engage learners. Training that allows learners to participate through practice opportunities is one way to make the learning experience more engaging. Training programs that only involve lectures encourage minimal levels of engagement, and adding interactivity is a good way to motivate learners to focus on, attend to, and engage in the training. For example, separating lectures with role playing exercises can help learners stay motivated and focused, and allow a chance for learners to interact with teammates and the instructor (Salas, DeRouin, & Littrell, 2005).

**Goal orientation**—or the degree to which one's goals are focused on either continual improvement of core competencies or objective, discrete metrics of performance—can have a big influence on the effectiveness of team training. Research suggests that the ideal goal orientation for team training should be "mastery orientation"—in other words, the instructional content and learning objectives of team training should be framed to motivate learners to focus on improving teamwork and/or taskwork skills, competencies, knowledge, or attitudes, rather than strict task performance (Bedwell & Salas, 2010). The training developer and/or facilitator can impact the learner's engagement by setting objectives of mastering the skill in the training intervention rather than focusing on performance. For example, instead of focusing on making the correct decisions and actions, the training can focus on emphasizing how to conduct effective decision making within a specific work context.

Motivation is also impacted by the degree of control that learners have during team training. For example, learners may be more motivated to participate if they are given the choice as to when the intervention will occur. Mathieu, Tannenbaum, and Salas (1992) found that learners were more motivated about training if given the opportunity to voluntarily attend the intervention. Establishing buy-in from those that will directly participate in team training is important for motivational and learning purposes in the long run. The perceived value of team training is also a major motivational component. Salas, Derouin, and Littrell (2005) indicated that the learner's ability to perceive the benefits of training and how it transfers to the real world context positively impacts a learner's motivation. Additionally, showing how the training will be positive for the organization and the learners themselves can help in motivating learners to participate. Training developers and facilitators should therefore take care to intentionally design elements of the team training that offer tangible and desirable benefits to learners; furthermore, training facilitators should make it a point to communicate these benefits to learners during training, so as to maintain consistently high levels of motivation throughout training.

**TIPS AND ADVICE**

- Incorporate interactivity into team training; do not just lecture or present materials (i.e., training is not one-way).
- Offer trainees control over aspects of instruction, such as when and where they are trained and the amount of practice they receive.
- Incorporate opportunities for trainees to interact with each other as well as with the instructor(s).
- Leverage multiple training media (e.g., graphics, text, video) to deliver content; ensure content and delivery are as engaging as possible.
- Design the training system to allow for exploring, navigating, and predicting future system states by the trainee.

Adapted from: Gregory et al., 2013; Sims, Salas, & Burke, 2005.

## Guideline 26: Match the Characteristics of the Learning Environment to Those of the Transfer Environment[15]

Effective team training ensures that instructional content matches the KSAs needed on the job. Matching content is essential because it facilitates transfer of learning in the training environment to the actual job performance setting. This includes matching teamwork KSAs covered by training to the behaviors and processes that the teams conduct in the work environment. For example, team training could focus on, and effectively improve a team's communication abilities; however, if the job requires only minimal communication but substantial conflict management, the training will not have been effective at improving team performance. Ultimately, it is more important to ensure that the instructional content taps into what the trainees are required to know to perform rather than obtaining the most advanced or sophisticated methods of delivering the training. This is similarly important involving the practice scenarios that learners conduct during training.

The selection of team training equipment and content involves the distinction between physical and psychological fidelity. **Physical fidelity** involves how the characteristics of the training environment match the actual workplace environment (e.g., mock-up of an airplane cockpit). **Psychological fidelity** refers to the replication of the KSAs used in the job environment within the training environment (e.g., similar patterns of coordination or back-up behaviors) (Bowers & Jentsch, 2001). Simulation and training interventions with high degrees of physical fidelity tend to be intriguing and attractive, and physical fidelity is indeed important for learning skills related to motor tasks or specific procedures. However, psychological fidelity is most critical for learning teamwork skills and behaviors. It is therefore essential that training developers—especially when selecting practice platforms for *teamwork* training—resist the temptation to select training delivery systems and interventions simply based on physical fidelity or how advanced the technology is; rather they must investigate the teamwork KSAs that the platform elicits from team members.

Training interventions are also an excellent opportunity for practicing on-the-job skills and tasks in a risk-free environment, and can be very useful for learning cases that may not occur frequently in the real world or cases that have critical consequences (e.g., emergency situations, complex flight procedures). For example, simulation-based training can replicate tasks and environments similar to the transfer environment and can produce different kinds of scenarios that learners may experience on the job (Salas, Wildman, & Piccolo, 2009). In such cases, simulations provide an opportunity to safely practice teamwork competencies and skills outside of the workplace (Kosarzycki, Salas, DeRouin, & Fiore, 2003).

---

### TIPS AND ADVICE

- Prioritize teamwork competencies over physical realism and aesthetics of the team training technology: Don't get caught up in fancy technology gimmicks!
- Ensure that the complexity, knowledge, and technical requirements of team training technology do not detract from learning.
- Ensure that team training requires the same KSAs required on the job.
- Ensure that the team's control and flexibility during team training does not differ greatly from what is inherent in the workplace.
- Incorporate details when creating the team training environment that reflect the real situational context on the job, such as tools, features, and constraints that would occur in natural operational settings.

Adapted from: Bowers & Jentsch, 2001; Kozlowski & Deshon, 2004; Salas, Bowers, & Rhodenizer, 2010.

---

## Guideline 27: Make Sure Trainees Are Capable of Using Team Training Technology

In addition to selecting technology and platforms that can deliver team training effectively, it is also important to consider whether the platform will be usable for those interacting with it. This is because despite how advanced and realistic a simulation platform may be—and regardless of its psychological fidelity—the best training platform in the world is essentially useless if it is so excessively

> The best training platform in the world is essentially useless if it is so excessively difficult to learn or operate that learners become unwilling to use it.

difficult to learn or operate that learners become unwilling to use it. Therefore, the usability factor regarding technology for training purposes needs to be taken into account when selecting the right platform and to provide proper training for interacting with the training tools. This means that not only should the selected platform actually *be* usable, but learners should *perceive* this usefulness as well.

When selecting the right team training technology, it is necessary to consider the skills and abilities of the learners who will be participating in training as they relate to working with the training technology. For example, if team training will be provided on a computer-based platform, the learner should have some experience with computers to operate the interface sufficiently (Salas, DeRouin, & Littrell, 2005). Therefore, it is important to consider whether the knowledge or skills required to use team training technology preclude some or all learners from using it. On the other hand, gaps in such knowledge and skills can be overcome with specialized training targeting how to use the technology (that is separate from team training). Instructors can ask learners to complete a brief proficiency test prior to team training to determine whether requisite technology skills are needed (Salas, DeRouin, & Littrell, 2005).

---

### TIPS AND ADVICE

- Consider the trainees' technical proficiency, the subject matter, and learning curve of content to determine if the use of team training technology is appropriate
- Allow trainees to practice with technology in order to develop prerequisite technology skills before using it in team training.

Adapted from: Sims et al., 2008.

---

## Guideline 28: Consider Short- and Long-Term Costs of Team Training Technology[16]

It is important to note that technology alone will not contribute to effective team training (Oser, Salas, Merket, & Bowers, 2001). Technology does not trump content—reading team training information on a computer screen versus a physical printout will more than likely lead to equivalent levels of learning. Nonetheless, the accessibility and operability of team training technology is one factor to consider when selecting a team training delivery medium. Does the training technology require a facilitator or operator? Will this person need to be external to the organization, or can an employee be trained to facilitate the program (and how long will training the facilitator take)? Does the team training technology require physical resources such as dedicated training space or physical simulation consoles—or can the training be conducted remotely using networked computers? Will there be ongoing costs (e.g., subscription fees, user licenses) for any purchased training software? There is a wide array of training tools available for training teamwork skills that cover the different methods of the training of information, demonstration, practice, and feedback. Investigating the cost and availability of these tools is essential for such decisions (Salas et al., 2009). For example, off-the-shelf software may be more accessible compared to high-fidelity simulations, and may also be a better alternative for integrating into existing training delivery structures. Of course, cost is only one monetary factor to take into consideration—estimating the return on investment (ROI) is also essential. Inexpensive training technology that doesn't yield results will have a much lower ROI than costly technology that actually results in learning and behavior change, especially if the trained teamwork competencies are of great organizational importance.

---

## TIPS AND ADVICE

- Don't get caught up on the price tag or the excitement of new technology—make sure it's appropriate and beneficial for your organization in the long run.
- Think about all the possible types of factors that training technology could impact and try to assign a value to these factors. Adding up the total cost/profit will provide an estimate of the long-term monetary benefits of training technology and help you make a decision about the practicality of investing in it.

Adapted from: Beaubien & Baker, 2004; Kozlowski & DeShon, 2004.

---

### Guideline 29: Establish the Organizational Infrastructure Needed to Support Team Training Technology[17]

A part of selecting team training technology is to ensure the organization has enough resources to operate and maintain the used platforms. Preparation and confirmation of what resources are required and available help in avoiding situations where the proper or entire team training cannot be delivered to learners for technical and/or logistical reasons (e.g., no available workstations, training tools not accessible during the scheduled training time, malfunctioning equipment, etc.). This includes having a sufficient amount of instructors, equipment, training materials, space to deliver training, and an adequate amount of time devoted to training (Salas et al., 2009). Lecture-based instructional content may be conducted utilizing basic technology in a classroom setting, but in cases where multiple computers are needed for learners, adequate resources are required for operating the equipment, such as having enough computers for learners that are participating, having enough power outlets for all computers to be functional, and having Internet access if the simulation is operated on a network structure. It is also important to make sure that the training area is comfortable for the learners, as this may affect the learners' motivation to participate (Guideline 25) (Salas, Wilson, Burke, Wightman, & Howse, 2006). Further, learners must have adequate time to participate in the training intervention; recall that respecting the time of the learners can positively aid in motivating the learner to participate in the team training process.

---

## TIPS AND ADVICE

- Find the space for team training technology—get creative if necessary.
- Inventory available resources to see if additional support systems are needed.
- Determine hardware and software requirements.
- Make sure the space selected for team training does not conflict with normal organizational operations.
- Consider the special needs for team training—for example, if your program requires lots of computers, make sure the scheduled location has appropriate ventilation and power outlets.
- Ensure there is adequate network capacity and security to support online exercises.
- Ensure that the team training facility is comfortable.
- Arrange for team training to take place during paying hours and schedule it so that trainees do not become overloaded or fall behind in their work because of team training.
- Secure a designated space for team training.
- Respect employees' time by being punctual with when team training begins and ends during a workday.

Adapted from: Salas et al., 2009; Salas et al., 2010.

---

## Principle 9: Ensure Instructors Are Prepared to Teach[18]

An important part of team training delivery is the role of the facilitator or instructor that actually interacts with the learners. Trainers/facilitators/instructors are the individuals that directly interact with the learners by introducing instructional content through lectures and demonstrations, monitoring the performance of learners during practice scenarios, and providing feedback. As instructors are responsible for the implementation of team training, they must be equipped with the tools and resources essential to training success.

## Guideline 30: Create Materials to Aid Instructors During Team Training[19]

Trainees are not the only individuals that can use materials and reference guides to facilitate learning. Instructors can be given reminders of practice scenarios that learners participate in during the training intervention. Scenario outlines can help instructors follow and anticipate key events during practice and monitor the learners' progress towards their goals. This is especially important in cases where they may experience high workload or are busy with multiple tasks. If instructors are provided materials to help monitor practice scenarios, they can better focus on the learners' performance and less on the characteristics or technical aspects of the practice scenario (Prince, Salas, Brannick, & Orasanu, 2005). Materials for the trainer should include procedures for providing the instructional content, a timeline to keep track of the team training program, and contingency plans in the case of unexpected situations (e.g., technical issues). To help provide feedback following team training, instructors can be provided with an outline of how to discuss performance, which will help keep the debrief structured and mitigate the possibility that important feedback components are overlooked.

---

**TIPS AND ADVICE**

- Create a training package for instructors that includes all the materials instructors will need to successfully provide information to trainees, demonstrate KSAs, facilitate learner practice opportunities, and provide feedback.
- Outline the team training program content.
- Provide instructors with a team training schedule that articulates the flow of training events with estimated timelines.
- Create tools to facilitate the measurement of teamwork processes (e.g., event-based score sheets) as well as the delivery of performance-based feedback (see also Principle 10).
- Provide training aids for instructors to serve as a reminder of information to present and reference during team training.

Adapted from: Ford et al., 1998.

---

## Guideline 31: Train Instructors

> Having expert knowledge of a job or workplace does not necessarily translate to being able to effectively train or instruct others.

It is important to note that having expert knowledge of a job or workplace does not necessarily translate to being able to effectively train or instruct others. While it is possible that trainers may be experts of the job or task being trained, they may have their own established methods or procedures for conducting the trained tasks. Occasionally, these idiosyncratic approaches may not be the optimal approach for learners, or they may simply not be how the job was intended to be conducted by the team (DeRouin, Parrish, & Salas, 2005). Therefore, training should also be provided to instructors to facilitate their ability to teach and monitor/measure learning (Dwyer & Salas, 2000; Salas et al., 2010). To this end, training facilitators should be allowed time to review the instructional content ahead of team training, coached to effectively detect good and poor performance, and taught how to provide effective feedback to the learners. Allowing trainers to practice playing the role of instructor and giving feedback can help refine their skills (Prince et al., 2005).

---

### TIPS AND ADVICE

- Brief instructors on the purpose, focus, and objectives of team training.
- Familiarize instructors with training materials and process before administering team training.
- Ensure instructors are able to discriminate between good and bad performance.
- Educate instructors on how to adjust the flow of information delivered to the trainee and guide learning.
- Prepare instructors to provide adequate and appropriate feedback to trainees.

Adapted from: Towler & Arman, 2013; Towler & Dipboye, 2001.

---

## Notes

1  Kraiger, 2003; Kraiger & Ford, 2007; Noe, 2002; Salas & Cannon-Bowers, 2001; Salas et al., 2012; Salas & Stagl, 2009; Salas, Wildman, & Piccolo, 2009
2  Kozlowski & Salas, 2010; Noe, 2002
3  Goldstein & Ford, 2002; Noe, 2002
4  Hoffman, 1999; Salas & Cannon-Bowers, 2000b
5  Salas, Burke, & Cannon-Bowers, 2002; Salas & Cannon-Bowers, 2000b

6  Noe, 2002
7  Beard, Salas, & Prince, 1995 Noe, 2002; Salas & Cannon-Bowers, 2000a
8  See more general information in Guideline 19.
9  Gregory et al., 2013; Salas & Cannon-Bowers, 2000b; Salas & Rosen, 2008
10 Bandura, 1977; Bandura, 1986; Gregory et al., 2013; Rosen et al., 2008
11 Cannon-Bowers et al., 1998; Grossman & Salas, 2011; Quiñones, 1997
12 Kluger & DeNisi, 1996; Salas & Cannon-Bowers, 1997; Smith-Jentsch, Zeisig, Acton, & McPherson, 1998
13 Salas & Cannon-Bowers, 2000b; Noe, 2002; Salas et al., 2012
14 See also Guideline 10; Salas & Cannon-Bowers, 2000a; Gregory et al., 2013.
15 Grossman & Salas, 2011; Salas et al., 2012; Noe, 2002
16 See also Guideline 5.
17 See also Guideline 5; Salas et al., 2009.
18 Towler & Arman, 2013; Towler & Dipboye, 2001
19 Ford et al., 1998

# References

Aguinis, H., & Kraiger, K. (2009). Benefits of training and development for individuals and teams, organizations, and society. *Annual Review of Psychology, 60,* 451–474.

Astin, A. W. (1984). Student involvement: A developmental theory for higher education. *Journal of College Student Personnel, 25*(4), 297–308.

Baldwin, T. T., Magjuka, R. J., & Loher, B. T. (1991). The perils of participation: Effects of choice of training on trainee motivation and learning. *Personnel Psychology, 44,* 51–65.

Bandura, A. (1977). *Social learning theory.* Englewood Cliffs, NJ: Prentice Hall.

Bandura, A. (1986). *Social foundations of thought and action: A social cognitive theory.* Rockville, MD: National Institutes of Mental Health.

Bandura, A. (1991). Social cognitive theory of self-regulation. *Organizational Behavior and Human Decision Processes, 50,* 248–287.

Beard, R. L., Salas, E., & Prince, C. (1995). Enhancing transfer of training: Using role-play to foster teamwork in the cockpit. *The International Journal of Aviation Psychology, 5*(2), 131–143.

Beaubien, J. M., & Baker, D. P. (2004). The use of simulation for training teamwork skills in health care: How low can you go? *Quality and Safety in Health Care, 13,* i51–i56.

Bedwell, W. L., & Salas, E. (2010). Computer-based training: Capitalizing on lessons learned. *International Journal of Training and Development, 14,* 239–249.

Boud, D., & Falchikov, N. (2006). Aligning assessment with long-term learning. *Assessment and Evaluation in Higher Education, 31*(4), 399–413.

Bowers, C. A., & Jentsch, F. (2001). Use of commercial, off-the-shelf, simulations for team research. In E. Salas (Ed.), *Advances in human performance and cognitive engineering research* (Vol. 1, pp. 293–317). Oxford, UK: Elsevier.

Burke, C. S., Salas, E., Wilson-Donnelly, K. A., & Priest, K. A. (2004). How to turn a team of experts into an expert medical team: Guidance from the aviation and military communities. *Quality in Health Care, 13,* i96–i104.

Burke, L. A., & Hutchins, H. M. (2007). Training transfer: An integrative literature review. *Human Resource Development Review, 6,* 263–296.

Cannon-Bowers, J. A., Rhodenizer, L., Salas, E., & Bowers, C. A. (1998). A framework for understanding pre-practice conditions and their impact on learning. *Personnel Psychology, 51,* 291–320.

Cannon-Bowers, J. A., Tannenbaum, S. I., Salas, E., & Volpe, C. E. (1995). Defining team competencies and establishing team training requirements. In R. Guzzo & E. Salas (Eds.) *Team effectiveness and decision making in organizations* (pp. 333–380). San Francisco, CA: Jossey-Bass.

Cierniak, G., Scheiter, K., & Gerjects, P. (2008). Explaining the split-attention effect: Is the reduction of extraneous cognitive load accompanied by an increase in germane cognitive load? *Computers in Human Behavior, 25,* 315–324.

DeRouin, R. E., Parrish, T. J., & Salas, E. (2005). On-the-job training: Tips for ensuring success. *Ergonomics in Design, 13,* 23–26.

Dwyer, D. J., & Salas, E. (2000). Principles of performance measurement for ensuring aircrew training effectiveness. In H. F. O'Neil Jr. & D. H. Andrews (Eds.), *Aircrew training and assessment* (pp. 223–244). Mahwah, NJ: Lawrence Erlbaum Associates.

Ellis, S., & Davidi, I. (2005). After-event reviews: Drawing lessons from successful and failed experience. *Journal of Applied Psychology, 90,* 857–871.

Ford, J. K., Smith, E. M., Weissbein, D. A., Gully, S. M., & Salas, E. (1998). Relationships of goal-orientation, metacognitive activity, and practice strategies with learning outcomes and transfer. *Journal of Applied Psychology, 83,* 218–233.

Franks, J. J., Bilbrey, C. W., Lien, K. G., & McNamara, T. P. (2000). Transfer-appropriate processing (TAP) and repetition priming. *Memory and Cognition, 28*(7), 1140–1151.

Goldstein, I. L., & Ford, J. K. (2002). *Training in organizations* (4th ed.). Belmont, CA: Wadsworth Thompson Learning.

Gregory, M. E., Feitosa, J., Driskell, T., Salas, E., & Vessey, W. B. (2013). Designing, delivering, and evaluating team training in organizations: Principles that work. In E. Salas, S. I. Tannenbaum, D. Cohen, & G. Latham (Eds.), *Developing and enhancing teamwork in organizations: Evidence-based best practices and guidelines* (pp. 441–487). San Francisco, CA: Jossey-Bass.

Grossman, R., & Salas, E. (2011). The transfer of training: What really matters. *International Journal of Training and Development, 15*(2), 103–120.

Hoffman, T. (1999). The meaning of competency. *Journal of European Industrial Training, 23*(6), 275–286.

Ilgen, D. R., Fisher, C. D., & Taylor, M. S. (1979). Consequences of individual feedback on behavior in organizations. *Journal of Applied Psychology, 64,* 349–371.

Khan, W. A. (1990). Psychological conditions of personal engagement and disengagement at work. *Academy of Management Journal, 33,* 692–724.

Kirschner, P. A. (2002). Cognitive load theory: Implications of cognitive load theory on the design of learning. *Learning and Instruction, 12*(1), 1–10.

Kluger, A. N., & DeNisi, A. (1996). The effects of feedback interventions on performance: A historical review, a meta-analysis, and a preliminary feedback intervention theory. *Psychological Bulletin, 119*(2), 254–284.

Komaki, J., Heinzmann, A. T., & Lawson, L. (1980). Effect of training and feedback: Component analysis of a behavioral safety program. *Journal of Applied Psychology, 65,* 261–270.

Kosarzycki, M. P., Salas, E., DeRouin, R., & Fiore, S. M. (2003). Distance learning in organizations: A review and assessments of future needs. In D. Stone (Ed.), *Advances in human performance and cognitive engineering research: Human resources technology* (pp. 69–98). New York, NY: JAI Press.

Kozlowski, S. W. J., & DeShon, R. P. (2004). A psychological fidelity approach to simulation-based training: Theory, research, and principles. In E. Salas, L. R. Elliot, S. G. Schflett, & M. D. Coovert (Eds.), *Scaled worlds: Development, validation, and applications* (pp. 75–99). Burlington, VT: Ashgate.

Kozlowski, S. W.J., & Salas E. (Eds.). (2010). *Learning, training, and development in organizations*. New York, NY: Taylor & Francis Group.

Kraiger, K. (2003). Perspectives on training and development. In W. C. Borman, D.R. Ilgen, & R.J. Klimoski (Eds.), *Handbook of psychology: Vol. 12 Industrial and organizational psychology* (pp. 171–192). Hoboken, NJ: Wiley.

Kraiger, K., & Ford,J. (2007). The expanding role of workplace training: Themes and trends influencing training research and practice. In L.L. Koppes (Ed.), *Historical perspectives in industrial and organizational psychology* (pp. 281–309). Mahwah, NJ: Lawrence Erlbaum Associates Publishers.

Kraiger, K., McLinden, D., & Casper, W. J., (2004). Collaborative planning for training impact. *Human Resource Management, 43*(4), 337–351.

Mathieu, J. E., Tannenbaum, S. I., & Salas, E. (1992). Influence of individual and situational characteristics on measures of training effectiveness. *Academy of Management Journal, 35*, 828–847.

Noe, R.A. (2002). *Employee training and development.* (2nd ed.). Boston, MA: McGraw-Hill/ Irwin.

Noe, R. A., & Colquitt, J. A. (2002). Planning for training impact: Principles of training effectiveness. In K. Kraiger (Ed.), *Creating, implementing, and maintaining effective training and development: State-of-the-art lessons for practice* (pp. 53–79). San Francisco, CA: Jossey-Bass.

Oser, R. L., Cannon-Bowers, J. A., Salas, E., & Dwyer, D. J. (1999). Enhancing human performance in technology-rich environments: Guidelines for scenario-based training. In E. Salas (Ed.), *Human/Technology interaction in complex systems* (Vol. 9, pp. 175–202). Greenwich, CT: JAI Press.

Oser, R. L., Salas, E., Merket, D. C., & Bowers, C.A. (2001). Applying resource management training in naval aviation: A methodology and lessons learned. In E. Salas, C. A. Bowers, & E. Edens (Eds.), *Improving teamwork in organizations: Applications of resource management training* (pp. 283–301). Mahwah, NJ: Lawrence Erlbaum Associates.

Patel, L. (2010). *ASTD state of the industry report 2010.* Alexandria, VA: American Society for Training & Development.

Priest, H. A., Wilson-Donnelly, K. A., Burke, C. S., Salas, E., Wears, R. L., & Perry, S. J. (2004). Human error, technology, and patient safety: Guidelines for the implementation of new technology into medical environments. Paper presented at the *Safety Across High-Consequence Industries Conference*, St. Louis, MO.

Prince, C., & Salas, E. (1999). Team processes and their training in aviation. In D. Garland, J. Wise, & D. Hopkins (Eds.), *Handbook of aviation human factors* (pp. 193–213). Mahwah, NJ: Lawrence Erlbaum Associates.

Prince, C., Salas, E., Brannick, M., & Orasanu, J. (2005). Beyond facilitation: An improved CRM debrief for safety training. *Human Factors and Aerospace Safety, 5*(1), 1–22.

Quiñones, M.A. (1995). Pretraining context effects: Training assignment as feedback. *Journal of Applied Psychology, 80*(2), 226–238.

Quiñones, M. A. (1997). Contextual influences on training effectiveness. In M. A. Quiñones & A. Ehrenstein (Eds.), *Training for a rapidly changing workplace: Applications of psychological research* (pp. 177–199). Washington, DC: American Psychological Association.

Rosen, M.A., Salas, E., Pavlas, D., Jensen, R., Fu, D., & Lampton, D. (2010). Demonstration-based training: A review of instructional features. *Human Factors, 52*, 596–609.

Rosen, M. A., Salas, E., Silvestri, S., Wu, T., & Lazzara, E. H. (2008). A measurement tool for simulation-based training in emergency medicine: The simulation module for assessment of resident targeted event responses (SMARTER) approach. *Simulation in Healthcare, 3*(3), 170–179.

Salas, E., Almeida, S. A., Salisbury, M., King, H., Lazzara, E. H., Lyons, R., . . . McQuillan, R. (2009). What are the critical success factors for team training in health care? *The Joint Commission Journal on Quality and Patient Safety, 35*, 398–405.

Salas, E., Bowers, C. A., & Rhodenizer, L. (2010). It is not how much you have but how you use it: Toward a rational use of simulation to support aviation training. *The International Journal of Aviation Psychology, 8*(3), 197–208.

Salas, E., Burke, C. S., & Cannon-Bowers, J. A. (2002). What we know about designing and delivering team training: Tips and guidelines. In K. Kraiger (Ed.), *Creating, implement-ing, and managing effective training and development: State-of-the-art lessons for practice* (pp. 234–259). San Francisco, CA: Jossey-Bass.

Salas, E., & Cannon-Bowers, J. A. (1997). Methods, tools, and strategies for team training. In M. A. Quinones & A. Ehrenstein (Eds.), *Training for a rapidly changing workplace: Applications of psychological research* (pp. 249–279). Washington, DC: American Psychological Association.

Salas, E., & Cannon-Bowers, J. A. (2000a). The anatomy of team training. In S. Tobias & J. D. Fletcher (Eds.), *Training & retraining: A handbook for business, industry, government, and the military* (pp. 312–335). New York, NY: Macmillan Reference USA.

Salas, E., & Cannon-Bowers, J. A. (2000b). Designing training systems systematically. In E. A. Locke (Ed.), *The Blackwell handbook of principles of organizational behavior* (pp. 43–59). Malden, MA: Blackwell Publisher.

Salas, E., & Cannon-Bowers, J. A. (2001). The science of training: A decade of progress. *Annual Review of Psychology, 52*, 471–499.

Salas, E., Cannon-Bowers, J. A., Rhodenizer, L., & Bowers, C. A. (1999). Training in orga-nizations: Myths, misconceptions, and mistaken assumptions. *Research in Personnel and Human Resources Management, 17*, 123–161.

Salas, E., Cannon-Bowers, J. A., & Smith-Jentsch, K. A. (2006). Principles and strategies for team training. In W. Karwowski (Ed.), *International encyclopedia of ergonomics and human factors* (Vol. 2, pp. 2245–2248). London, UK: Taylor & Francis.

Salas, E., DeRouin, R. E., & Littrell, L. N. (2005). Research-based guidelines for design-ing distance learning: What we know so far. In H. G. Guetal & D. L. Stone (Eds.), *The brave new world of eHR: Human resources management in the digital age* (pp. 104–137). San Francisco, CA: Jossey-Bass.

Salas, E., Klein, C., King, H., Salisbury, M., Augenstein, J. S., Birnbach, D. J., . . . Upshaw, C. (2008). Debriefing medical teams: 12 evidence-based best practices and tips. *The Joint Commission Journal on Quality and Patient Safety, 34*(9), 518–527.

Salas, E., Oser, R. L., Cannon-Bowers, J. A., & Daskarolis-Kring, E. (2002). Team training in virtual environments: An event-based approach. In K. M. Stanney (Ed.), *Handbook of virtual environments: Design, implementation, and applications* (pp. 873–892). Mahwah, NJ: Lawrence Erlbaum Associates.

Salas, E., Priest, H. A., Wilson, K. A., & Burke, C. S. (2006). Scenario-based training: Improv-ing military mission performance and adaptability. In T. W. Britt, A. B. Adler, & C. A. Castro (Eds.), *Military life: The psychology of serving in peace and combat* (Vol. 2, pp. 32–53). Westport, CT: Praeger Security International.

Salas, E., & Rosen, M. A. (2008). Beyond the bells and whistles: When simulation-based team training works best. *Forum, 26*(4), 6–7.

Salas, E., Rosen, M. A., & King, H. B. (2009). Integrating teamwork into the "DNA" of graduate medical education: Principles for simulation-based training. *Journal of Graduate Medical Education, 1*(2), 243–244.

Salas, E., Rosen, M. A., Weaver, S. J., Held, J. D., & Weissmuller, J. J. (2010). Research on SBT leads to the development of guidelines applicable to diverse training scenarios. *Ergonomics in Design, 17,* 12–18.

Salas, E., Sims, D., Klein, C., & Burke, C.S. (2003). How to turn a team of experts into an expert team. *Forum, 23*(3), 8–9.

Salas, E., & Stagl, K. C. (2009). Design training systematically and follow the science of training. In E. A. Locke (Ed.), *Handbook of principles of organizational behavior: Indispensable knowledge for evidence-based management* (2nd ed., pp. 59–83). West Sussex, UK: John Wiley & Sons.

Salas, E., Tannenbaum, S. I., Kraiger, K., & Smith-Jentsch, K. A. (2012). The science of training and development in organizations: What matters in practice. *Psychological Science in the Public Interest, 13*(2), 74–101.

Salas, E., Wildman, J. L., & Piccolo, R. F. (2009). Using simulation-based training to enhance management education. *Academy of Management Learning and Education, 8*(4), 559–573.

Salas, E., Wilson, J.R., Burke, C. S., Wightman, D., & Howse, W. R. (2006). Crew resource management training research, practice, and lessons learned. *Reviews of Human Factors and Ergonomics, 2,* 35–73.

Salas, E., Wilson, J. R., & Lyons, R. (2008). Designing and delivering training for multi-cultural interactions in organizations. In D. Stone & E. F. Stone-Romero (Eds.), *Cultural diversity and human resource practices* (pp. 115–134). Mahwah, NJ: Lawrence Erlbaum Associates.

Salas, E., Wilson, J. R., Priest, H. A., & Guthrie, J. (2006). Training in organizations: The design, delivery, and evaluation of training systems. In G. Salvendy (Ed.), *Handbook of human factors and ergonomics* (pp. 472–512). Hoboken, NJ: John Wiley & Sons.

Salas, E., Wilson, K.A., Burke, C. S., & Priest, H.A. (2005). Using simulation-based training to improve patient safety: What does it take? *The Joint Commission Journal on Quality and Patient Safety, 31*(7), 363–371.

Salas, E., Wilson, K.A., Burke, C. S., Wightman, D. C., & Howse, W. R. (2006). A checklist for crew resource management training. *Ergonomics in Design, 14,* 6–15.

Schmidt, R.A., & Wulf, G. (1997). Continuous concurrent feedback degrades skill learning: Implications for training and simulation. *Human Factors, 39,* 509–525.

Sims, D. E., Burke, C. S., Metcalf, D. S., & Salas, E. (2008). Research-based guidelines for designing blended learning. *Ergonomics in Design, 16*(1), 23–29.

Sims, D. E., Salas, E., & Burke, C. S. (2005). Promoting effective team performance through training. In S.E. Wheelan (Ed.), *The handbook of group research and practice* (pp. 407–425). London, UK: SAGE Publications.

Smith-Jentsch, K. A., Jentsch, F. G., Payne, S. C., & Salas, E. (1996). Can pretraining experiences explain individual differences in learning? *Journal of Applied Psychology, 81,* 110–116.

Smith-Jentsch, K. A., Zeisig, R. L., Acton, B., & McPherson, J. A. (1998). Team dimensional training: A strategy for guided team self-correction. In J. A. Cannon-Bowers & E. Salas (Eds.), *Making decisions under stress: Implications for individual and team training* (pp. 271–297). Washington, DC: American Psychological Association.

Surface, E.A. (2012). Training needs assessment: Aligning learning and capability with performance requirements and organizational objectives. In M.A. Wilson, W. Bennett, S. G. Gibson, & G. M. Alliger (Eds.), *The handbook of work analysis: Methods, systems, applications, and science of work measurement in organizations* (pp. 437–462). New York, NY: Routledge.

Sweller, J., van Merriënboer, J.J.G., & Paas, F.G.W.C. (1998). Cognitive architecture and instructional design. *Educational Psychology Review, 10*(3), 251–296.

Taylor, P. J., Russ-Eft, D. F., Chan, D.W.L. (2005) A meta-analytic review of behavior modeling training. *Journal of Applied Psychology, 90*(4), 692–709.

Towler, A., & Arman, G. (2013). Trainer communication style and training outcomes. In M.A. Paludi (Ed.), *Psychology for business success* (pp. 103–113). Santa Barbara, CA: Praeger.

Towler, A.J., & Dipboye, R.L. (2001). Effects of trainer expressiveness, organization, and trainee goal orientation on training outcomes. *Journal of Applied Psychology, 86*(4), 664–673.

Tharenou, P. (2001). The relationship of training motivation to participation in training and development. *Journal of Occupational and Organizational Psychology, 74*(5), 599–621.

Weaver, S. J., Wildman, J. L., & Salas, E. (2009). How to build expert teams: Best practices. In R. J. Burke & C. L. Cooper (Eds.), *The peak performing organization* (pp. 129–156). New York, NY: Routledge.

# 5

# PILLAR 4

## Evaluate the Team Training Program

**Is the training working? Was it successful?** Although evaluations are oftentimes an afterthought, they are integral for truly determining learners' teamwork and taskwork competencies, not to mention the effectiveness of the team training program itself. More specifically, evaluations systematically collect data to diagnosis both the strengths and weaknesses of individuals, teams, organizations, and the training program (Salas, Rosen, Burke, Nicholson, & Howse, 2007). These diagnostics are used to make judgments about the effectiveness of the program as well as improve its future iterations (Patton, 2008). Consequently, evaluation should be considered throughout the entire training process (i.e., development, implementation, and sustainment) as opposed to simply at the completion of the actual training. In fact, it may seem counterintuitive, but efficacious evaluations should ideally begin prior to training since they are time and resource intensive. Initiating evaluations during

**Top Reasons Organizations Neglect Evaluations (Russ-Eft & Preskill, 2009)**

1. Employees misunderstand the evaluation's purpose and role
2. Employees fear the results and impact of the evaluation
3. No one has expertise to conduct an evaluation
4. An evaluation was not requested
5. Employees think it will be too expensive and time and resource intensive
6. Top management thinks they already know the answers
7. Previous experiences have been poor
8. Employees don't value evaluations
9. Employees think the results won't be used

the preliminary stages of team training ensures that all facets of evaluations are examined beyond the actual metrics. That is, a comprehensive view of evaluations considers the following core questions: *What* will be measured, *how* will it be measured, *why* is it being measured, *when* will it be measured, and *who* is going to measure it? In essence, these answers will identify the team competencies that are targeted for measurement, the metrics that will be leveraged to assess the team competencies, the purpose for the measurement, the point(s) in time the measurement tools will be implemented, and which individual(s) will be utilizing the metrics.

As demonstrated by the aforementioned questions, evaluations are a system comprised of multiple, complex, and dynamic elements. However, the potential gains are worth the investment. Evaluations assist organizations in assuring quality, increasing knowledge, improving behaviors, prioritizing resources, delivering initiatives, instilling accountability, fostering marketing, and encouraging change—not to mention evincing and/or improving the overall effectiveness of training programs (Russ-Eft & Preskill, 2009). To achieve these advantageous and profitable outcomes, all of the key elements of evaluations must be carefully scrutinized. Simply stated, the effectiveness of team training is heavily dependent on thoughtful evaluations. The following principles, guidelines, and tips will provide assistance on how to unpack all of the complexities that are inherent when creating and executing team training evaluations.

## Principle 10: Determine What to Measure During Team Training and How You Will Measure It[1]

Determining what to measure and how it will be measured may seem simple; however, it is actually quite complex. In addition to selecting the actual measures and metrics of training effectiveness, the learners, assessors, environment, and curriculum all need to be considered. The following sections will elucidate how to appropriately scrutinize each of these critical elements.

### Guideline 32: Select Measures That Target Learning Objectives and KSAs, Diagnose Performance, and Inform Meaningful and Constructive Feedback[2]

Even though it can be commonplace to select measurement methods based on their convenience, it is essential to select measures that correspond to team competencies (Salas & Rosen, 2009). As discussed in the introduction, while there are many different ways of conceptualizing the various teamwork competencies, it has been suggested that there are at least nine components to effective teamwork outside of the taskwork itself (Salas, Shuffler, Thayer, Bedwell, & Lazzara, in press). Though heuristics and taxonomies help pare down the literature, making team competencies clearer and more parsimonious, it is neither feasible nor necessary to focus on every aspect of teamwork competencies for a team training program. Just as team training is not always the answer (see Pillar 1), or more complex technology does not always make for better training (see Guideline 26), it is neither necessary, desirable, nor possible to attempt to train every single team competency. Consequently, **strong team training should prioritize only that subset of team competencies that will yield the greatest impact on performance**.

In addition to broad team competencies, measures should also correspond to learning objectives as well as KSAs (Salas & Rosen, 2009). Learning objectives are more granular specifications of what the training curriculum is striving to instruct (Rosen, Salas, Silvestri, Wu, & Lazzara, 2008), and KSAs are the specific thoughts, behaviors, and attitudes a learner must possess or exhibit in order to evince that the desired objective has been accomplished (Rosen, Salas, Wilson, et al., 2008). The granularity of KSAs is particularly important for measurement, as it helps in the selection of highly targeted measures. These measures then enable assessors to determine whether a learner has demonstrated the targeted KSA appropriately. Additionally, granularity is also vital for providing specific, constructive, and diagnostic feedback for performance remediation. Ultimately, the selection of measures should be guided by: (1) the team competency that the training is focusing on, (2) the stated learning objectives of the program, and (3) the targeted team KSAs of the training. By selecting evaluation measures in this systematic fashion, training evaluators will be able to more clearly provide evidence of the effectiveness of the intervention and, when relevant, identify where training is not as effective so as to improve it in future iterations.

---

## TIPS AND ADVICE

- Ensure that measures align with the learning objectives of the team training.
- Specify how and why a particular measurement tool is being used.
- Detail what type of information the measurement tool elicits.
- Determine the appropriate time and place to measure KSAs.
- Identify who will be assessing performance.
- Include team training and subject matter experts in the measurement selection process.
- Know the pros and cons of all measurement tools and techniques.
- Ensure diagnostic measures are easy to use.
- Assure measures can capture a wide range of performance in a variety of settings.
- Allow measures to be flexible and substitutable.

- Align measurement format (e.g., accuracy, frequency, quantity, etc.) to the type of teamwork being assessed.
- Tailor tools for timely, specific feedback.
- Design measures in parallel with practice activities.

Adapted from: Salas, Rosen, Weaver, Held, & Weissmuller, 2009.

## Guideline 33: Develop Benchmarks of Learning and Performance to Assess Teamwork KSAs at Many Points Throughout Team Training—Including Before Team Training[3]

Benchmarks are essentially a depiction of the ideal levels of the KSAs targeted in training curricula (Salas et al., 2009). For example, training benchmarks could include attaining a score of 80% or higher on a safety skills knowledge test or completing a teamwork simulation while successfully exhibiting a predetermined level of trained teamwork KSAs. They simplify observations by serving as the standard that assessors can leverage to compare an individual's or team's performance. Having these benchmarks is particularly valuable for judging complex behaviors (Flin & Martin, 2001) because the process of evaluating complex behaviors often leads to biased or unreliable ratings. Because the process of measuring complex teamwork behaviors is so difficult, benchmarks that offer explicit guidance on how to identify ideal instances of trained KSAs behaviors should be leveraged.

These benchmarks should be appropriate and approved by organizational leaders and SMEs in the trained task. For example, the training developer may assume that 80% knowledge of a safety content domain is sufficient; however, task experts may review the benchmark and determine that 95% or even complete knowledge is mandatory for desirable team outcomes. Conversely, benchmarks may not always need to be restrictive in the sense of evidencing just one team competency or KSA. For example, a surgery team may need team training to improve their decision-making abilities in high-pressure situations. If it is determined that poor conflict management and coordination skills are undermining the team's performance, the training should focus on improving these competencies. The measurement strategy should not simply focus on improvements in the team's outcomes, but whether or not the team is improving in the targeted KSAs. Furthermore, multiple metrics of the targeted KSAs should be leveraged (e.g., declarative knowledge tests, behavioral checklists), in order to avoid the possibility of unreliable measures or metrics that do not sufficiently describe or measure the KSA of interest. Ultimately, developing benchmarks for multiple facets of the training fosters a more accurate depiction of the learner's ability (Littrell & Salas, 2005).

**TIPS AND ADVICE**

- Use information from organizational leaders and SMEs to establish the criteria for reaching appropriate benchmarks.
- Use numerous criteria to determine success or failure.

Adapted from: Salas et al., 2009.

### Guideline 34: Adopt Measures That Capture Both Teamwork Outcomes (e.g., Mission Completion, Products) and Teamwork Processes (e.g., Communication)[4]

Evaluations of team and team training effectiveness should target team outcomes to gain insights on *what happened* during a performance episode. Such outcomes are often assessed effectively with quantitative methodologies (e.g.,

> Assessing outcomes answers *what* happened.
> Assessing processes answers *why* it happened.

surveys and structured observations), which are helpful in establishing causal relationships between key variables within the team performance domain (Mack, Woodsong, MacQueen, Guest, & Namey, 2011). Furthermore, while understanding *what* happened (i.e., outcomes) is fundamental for improving future performance, understanding *why* it happened (i.e., processes) is equally—if not more—important. Simply knowing the outcome does not afford the ability to diagnose and remediate deficiencies (Salas et al., 2009), while understanding the reasons why an outcome occurred offers great insight for how to enhance performance, as this knowledge provides concrete directions for rectifying team performance issues (Salas, Cannon-Bowers, & Smith-Jentsch, 2006; Salas et al., 2009).

Inherently, quantitative techniques are less flexible than their qualitative counterparts. Quantitative metrics must necessarily operate within a predetermined set of numerical boundaries. This rigidity is advantageous for minimizing extraneous influences (e.g., rater bias) and targeting only desired outcomes. However, qualitative measurement techniques (e.g., interviews and focus groups), offer unique advantages as well. These techniques are designed to acquire rich, in-depth data about behaviors, values, opinions, and contexts (Mack et al., 2011). Accordingly, qualitative methods are often quite useful when assessing complex behaviors, thoughts, and feelings—especially when these things have not been previously placed neatly into validated, fully developed measures. Ultimately, both qualitative and quantitative measurement techniques are especially useful when used in combination—qualitative methods allow for the assessment of KSAs that may have been overlooked or are not easily quantified, while quantitative methods allow for rapid and systematic assessment and analysis.

Although there are facets of teamwork (e.g., communication and coordination) that are important for all teams irrespective of their tasks and environment, teams do not train and operate in isolation. Thus, it is also vital to develop measures that will target the idiosyncrasies within the team as well as the contextual factors that surround and impact the team (Kendall & Salas, 2004). Evaluating both generic and individualized team processes as well as team outcomes fosters a more accurate representation. Additionally, it ensures that teams are accomplishing the intended objectives, and that teams are progressing towards the objectives in an appropriate manner (Salas, Burke, & Fowlkes, 2006).

---

### TIPS AND ADVICE

- Include process measures to determine *why* something happened.
- Incorporate outcome measures to determine *what* happened.

Adapted from: Rosen, Salas, Silvestri, et al., 2008; Salas, Burke, & Cannon-Bowers, 2002

---

### Guideline 35: Utilize Several Measurement Sources, Techniques, and Tools to Capture Multiple Aspects of Performance[5]

Learning and performance, especially team performance, are complex and multifaceted. It is, therefore, unwise to assume that team process and performance—and the effectiveness of team training—can be measured with one simple measurement technique. Indeed, the only way to diagnose, deconstruct, and address every element of team performance or team training effectiveness is by leveraging multiple measurement sources, techniques, and tools (Salas et al., 2009). We address each of these in turn.

The **source of measurement** refers to *who* is conducting the assessment; these sources may be supervisors, peers, or even the learners themselves. Traditionally, supervisors tend to endorse summative assessments (i.e., high stakes, summary evaluations) more so than peers and/or subordinates, who are more suitable for conducting formative assessments (i.e., ongoing, developmental evaluations). Peers and subordinates, who typically interact with individuals on a more frequent basis than do supervisors, are well suited for providing valuable developmental insights and feedback for learners. Peer ratings are particularly important in team training, where the perceptions of peers (i.e., fellow teammates) heavily influence many team processes and outcomes. Finally, learners can also be valuable measurement sources, particularly when team training is guided by self-directed learning.

Beyond being classified as a supervisor, peer, or the self, sources may be described by their level of expertise. Experts may be valuable measurement sources, because they are necessarily more familiar with the task; however, expertise often brings with it greater responsibility, making experts less available for training. And while experts may be more capable of discriminating amongst effective and ineffective team behaviors and processes, expertise can be a double-edged sword. When experts attain a deep level of familiarity with a task, they may experience "automaticity," or the phenomenon of knowing something so intimately that it no longer requires conscious thought (Ford & Sterman, 1998; LaFrance, 1989; Ryder & Redding, 1993). When this occurs, it may be difficult for experts to effectively rate the nuances of effective performance unless systematic benchmarks are provided (see Guideline 33). Individuals with intermediate levels of task expertise may be less capable of discriminating amongst learner behaviors, but they are more adaptable and available for training. Novices, initially, will be the least capable at discriminating learner behaviors and will require the most training. However, research suggests that novices can be trained to make assessments relatively equivalent to experts (e.g., O'Byrne, Clark, & Malakuti, 1997). Consequently, the most appropriate source of measurement is contingent upon the purpose of the evaluation and the availability of time and resources.

The **techniques and tools** refer to the *how* and *what* is being used to conduct the evaluation. For example, surveys as well as observation and interview protocols are commonplace assessment tools. More specifically, rating scales, checklists, and frequency counts are highly utilized. Rating scales offer numerical or descriptive judgments of how well something was performed. Checklists simply rely on dichotomous responses (e.g., yes/no, performed/not performed). Frequency counts indicate the number of times something occurred. Rating scales can offer insights on the quality of how well something was performed, but due to the variety of possible ratings, these scales are more cognitively taxing for assessors. Conversely, frequency counts and checklists only provide evidence as to whether something happened. But, given the limited assessment options, frequency counts and checklists require less cognitive processing (Rosen, Salas, Silvestri, et al., 2008). Therefore, they are less burdensome on raters. Given this variation in mental workload, rating scales should be used by individuals with a nuanced perspective on the content to be assessed (e.g., experts, peers), while checklists may be more appropriate for individuals with a simpler understanding of the content (e.g., novices), who will require more thought to complete assessments.

Finally, evaluating both the team *and* its individual members is important, irrespective of the source, technique, or tool. Although team training primarily focuses on accelerating team KSAs, diagnosing specific individual member processes and outcomes is also important because some members may need specific, customized remediation (Salas et al., 2009). In sum, utilizing a multi-methodology evaluation approach enables the training developer and/or evaluator to identify the strengths and weaknesses of the team and the individuals who comprise the team by: (1) clearly and systematically measuring the essential determinants of performance, and (2) uncovering patterns and interrelationships between these determinants.

---

**TIPS AND ADVICE**

- Select tools that can assess performance objectively (e.g., timeliness, errors, etc.) and subjectively (e.g., surveys or expert ratings).
- Include assessments during training to quantify the development of teamwork KSAs (i.e., formative assessments) and to evaluate the proficiency of teamwork KSAs (i.e., summative assessments).
- Utilize measurement tools in a consistent manner.
- Use technology to aid in evaluation to automate measurement whenever possible.

Adapted from: Salas et al., 2009; Salas & Stagl, 2009.

---

## Guideline 36: Develop Measurement Tools to Assess Training Using Multiple Criteria[6]

As mentioned previously, evaluating multiple aspects of teamwork and team performance is essential for obtaining a confident evaluation of team training effectiveness. There are various taxonomies that offer guidance on training evaluation criteria (Alliger, Tannenbaum, Bennet Jr., Traver, & Shotland, 1997; Baldwin & Ford, 1988; Kirkpatrick, 1994; Klein, Sims, & Salas, 2006; Kraiger, Ford, & Salas, 1993). Although no taxonomy is perfect and may not apply to every circumstance or used without question, Kirkpatrick's (1994) framework is widely accepted. This multilevel evaluation framework includes reactions, learning, behaviors, and results. **Reactions** simply answer the question of whether the learners enjoyed the training. They are usually measured immediately after training using a survey. **Learning** provides insights as to whether the learners acquired the fundamental knowledge, or changed their attitudes and/or behaviors *in the context of the actual training setting*. It is typically assessed using a questionnaire administered immediately following training, though behavioral learning can also be gauged with observational rating scales. Meanwhile, assessing the level of **behaviors** indicates the degree to which learners are exhibiting the trained content *in the actual performance context*. One common methodology for assessing behaviors is structured observations. Structured observations can be ideal because they can determine the quantity (i.e., frequency) of exhibited behaviors as well as the quality of the behaviors. Finally, the **results** level indicates the extent that the training impacted the organization. Because outcomes are essentially determining the organization's bottom line, they are extremely context dependent. Undoubtedly, evaluating such outcomes and even behaviors can be more time and labor intensive compared to reactions and learning. But, as suggested previously, an accurate depiction of the impact of team training is contingent upon a multi-criteria evaluation.

---

### TIPS AND ADVICE

- Create tools to measure reactions, learning, behaviors, and outcomes.
- Don't ignore assessing trainee behaviors and organizational outcomes despite their difficulty.
- Measure more than just declarative knowledge to gauge learning.
- Measure teamwork continuously.

Adapted from: Kirkpatrick, 1994; Gregory, Feitosa, Driskell, Salas, & Vessey, 2013; Paris, Salas, & Cannon-Bowers, 2000; Rosen, Salas, Silvestri, et al., 2008.

---

## Guideline 37: Equip Assessors to Use Measurement Tools Correctly[7]

Assessors are frequently a fundamental component for conducting robust evaluations within team training, especially when the training is not self-directed or does not lend itself to automatic scoring. However, assessors need to be properly equipped—through rater training and the provision of any requisite materials—to utilize measurement tools optimally (Dwyer & Salas, 2000; Salas, 2006). Providing assessors with all of the necessary tools and skills for effective rating fosters more reliable and valid evaluations.

Clearly, assessors will need the actual metrics that they will be utilizing. These metrics should also come with a scoring guide. A scoring guide offers assessors direction on how to rate their observations accordingly. Scoring guides should include definitions of the core competencies, as well as explicit examples of the different types and variations of the competencies (Rosen et al., 2010). Structured measurement protocols with scoring guides are beneficial for assessors as they reduce the cognitive load associated with monitoring and rating by focusing assessors' attention on only the relevant and expected behaviors, rather than having to make decisions about what or how to measure (Salas & Cannon-Bowers, 2000; Salas & Rosen, 2009).

In addition to tools, assessors also need the appropriate skills. Therefore, they need to be trained to use the tool(s), monitor learners' progress, and actually make rating judgments (Dwyer & Salas, 2000; Salas et al., 2009). Such training will enable assessors to rate consistently, systematically, and with minimal bias (Salas,

Wilson, Priest, & Guthrie, 2006). Rating consistently becomes especially paramount when there are multiple assessors, which is often necessary given logistical and cognitive constraints (Salas et al., 2009). Using videotaped sessions of previous performances can serve as a useful training mechanism (Rosen et al., 2010).

---

**TIPS AND ADVICE**

- Train assessors on how to use measurement tools.
- Provide assessors with the necessary materials to apply measurement tools appropriately.
- Use multiple assessors for more accurate evaluations.
- Give assessors structured tools.
- Create a scoring guide for assessors to use and ensure the guides have definitions and examples of teamwork behaviors for reference.
- Don't overburden assessors with too many things or people to measure.
- Use videotaped sessions to provide assessors with practice using the tools.
- Pilot test measures to ensure they are used successfully.

Adapted from: Salas et al., 2009.

---

## Principle 11: Analyze *If* the Team Training Program Was Successful and Determine *Why* It Was Effective (or Not)

After monitoring and rating learning and performance within the team training context, team training evaluation data must be analyzed and interpreted. The interpretation of team training evaluation data will guide the next steps (i.e., sustainment, revisions, or broader dissemination) of the team training program.

### Guideline 38: Establish the Characteristics (i.e., Reliability and Validity) of the Measurement Tools by Utilizing Established Research and Statistical Methods[8]

The psychometric properties of team training evaluation measures (i.e., reliability and validity) are critical factors to take into account when analyzing evaluation data (Baker & Salas, 1997). Simply stated, **reliability** refers to consistency (of measurement), and **validity** refers to accuracy (of measurement). Expanding upon that, establishing the reliability ensures that tools are consistent across time and raters, and determining the validity assures that tools are measuring the intended team training competencies. It is important to note that reliability "caps" validity; in other words, a measure can only be valid to the extent that it

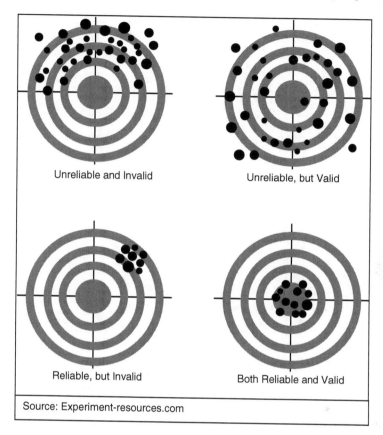

Unreliable and Invalid

Unreliable, but Valid

Reliable, but Invalid

Both Reliable and Valid

Source: Experiment-resources.com

**FIGURE 5.1.** Visual Depiction of Reliability and Validity.
*Source*: Experiment-resources.com

is also reliable. To illustrate this, refer to the example in the upper right corner of the associated figure. Though this hypothetical measure is considered "valid" in the sense that the unreliable measures happen to average out to the correct middle point, the error and unreliability associated with this particular tool means that inferences made are quite tenuous—especially when compared to a more reliable measure.

Reliability is also important in a practical sense. Team training often requires multiple observers to rate learners' progress as a result of the training (see Guideline 37). With less reliable measures, it may take a greater number of assessors to obtain a confident rating of learning or behavior change. The same is true of self-report rating scales—using more reliable and valid measures, means that raters do not have to respond to multiple related measures of similar constructs. In sum, both reliability and validity are important for determining the conclusions that can be extracted from evaluation data. However, this is only a very cursory review of these psychometric concepts—we therefore encourage readers to consult additional resources (e.g., Fleiss & Cohen, 1973; Shadish, Cook, & Campbell, 2002).

---

### TIPS AND ADVICE

- Establish the consistency of measurement tools over time and agreement across raters.
- Monitor the consistency periodically to identify changes and provide necessary changes.
- Ensure the tools are measuring what they are supposed to.
- Assure evaluation tools can predict scores on an established criterion.
- Identify extraneous factors that may be influencing team training evaluation findings.

Adapted from: Baker & Salas, 1997; Salas et al., 2009.

---

## Guideline 39: Account for Short- and Long-Term Performance Trends[9]

> Longitudinal evaluation of training effectiveness is important because knowledge naturally decays when it is not applied.

Another characteristic of effective team training measurement, analysis, and evaluation is identifying the effects of team training on essential aspects of team process (e.g., conflict management, communication, backing up behaviors) and performance over time. This is essential in part because knowledge naturally decays—especially when it is not applied due to lack of support, overwork, or a general lack of interest. Longitudinal measurement of training effectiveness is also uniquely important in the context of team training, as it may be acceptable for knowledge to decay and even dissipate in *some* team members. In other words, with team training, the primary unit of interest is the team—so long as the team is exhibiting trained teamwork and taskwork KSAs (and performance) over time, it may be appropriate to consider the training a success. On the other hand, monitoring trained teamwork and taskwork competencies over time may also help to determine when the team has reached critical levels of knowledge decay, necessitating refresher training. Collecting effectiveness data over time allows a more comprehensive analysis of the factors influencing teamwork and long-term training effectiveness. In addition, maintaining a database that collates all of the data will foster the ability to detect changes in specific individuals, teams, and the team training program.

**TIPS AND ADVICE**

- Create and use a database for fostering performance comparisons across time.
- Link performance data from team training to the larger database inventory to diagnose trends.
- Store data in a way that is easy to access and interpret.
- Evaluate teamwork before team training in order to link team training outcomes to future performance.

Adapted from: Gregory et al., 2013.

## Guideline 40: Document and Disseminate Evaluation Findings[10]

The basis of team training evaluation is identifying the strengths and weaknesses of the team training program and determining to what extent the training accomplished its targeted objectives (Shapiro et al., 2008). However, documenting and disseminating the effects of training is crucial. Such efforts guide the future of the training program. Any deficiencies in the training program warrant modifications, while successful training components may call for expansion and implementation in other organizational contexts. Accordingly, reporting on the effectiveness of team training is more than simply listing how learners changed as a result of the training. Reporting team training effectiveness is primarily concerned with three things: (1) identifying the *actual* effects of team training, (2) garnering continued buy-in from organizational leadership, and (3) improving the training program where necessary.

One of the most essential aspects of evaluating team training is being able to show organizational stakeholders how effective the training has been. As discussed in Guideline 36, assessing the effects of team training can be conducted on four levels: *reactions, learning, behaviors,* and *results* (Kirkpatrick, 1994). Each of these offer evidence of effectiveness in one way or another, and each have pros and cons associated with

*Learning* and *behavior* effectiveness metrics are especially important when establishing team training effectiveness for one major reason—when conducted correctly, they offer strong causal evidence for the efficacy of team training.

them. Reaction data is easy to collect and can provide good insights particularly for improving future iterations of team training. If learners are completely disengaged with a part or parts of training, this is valuable data for tweaking elements of the training moving forward. This notwithstanding, positive training reaction evaluations are typically not a major learning objective aligned with overarching organizational goals. In other words, positive reactions are largely meaningless if they are not accompanied by increases in learning, behavior, and, ideally, results.

Learning and behavior effectiveness metrics are especially important when establishing the effectiveness of team training for one major reason—when conducted correctly, they offer strong causal evidence for the efficacy of team training. As discussed in Guideline 39, longitudinal measurement is important, but at the very least, effective training evaluations should incorporate pre-training metrics of learners' targeted KSAs. These pre-training metrics should have already been obtained or collected during team training needs analysis (see Pillar 1). By using pre- and post-training metrics of effectiveness, the training evaluator can clearly point to the team training intervention as accounting for any changes from pre to post. One difference between learning and behavior metrics has to do with the tradeoffs associated with confidence of causal inferences versus the importance of apparent changes. That is, learning metrics offer more accurate estimates of training effects than behavioral ones, as they are collected during or immediately following training. Reducing the lag time between training and evaluation increases the confidence of causal inferences, as it reduces the possibility of other factors being the cause behind changes associated with training. On the other hand, learning metrics, which refer to changes that occurs *in the training environment*, are typically of less interest to organizational leadership than behavioral metrics, which refer to changes that are actually occurring *in the workplace and performance setting*. In other words, a team could learn and agree that conflict management is important, come to know how to do it, and possibly even manage conflict in some training simulations, but if this team fails to maintain these changes in the workplace, the organization may see this as a failed intervention. However, while behavior metrics are more apparently meaningful, the presence of confounding variables may reduce the confidence associated with these inferences. Consider, for example, in the team conflict management scenario above if the team returned to the workplace and immediately had to deal with potential outside sources of conflict (e.g., incorporate a new team member, increase in workload, organizational downsizing). If this were the case, the team's failure to exhibit conflict management behaviors might not mean that the training was ineffective, but that extraneous factors caused these effects. This illustrates the importance of having a systematic measurement plan in place that assesses multiple criteria—and also the importance of reporting these multiple criteria to organizational leadership.

At the risk of stating the obvious, once the efficacy of the team training is determined, this information must be presented to organizational leadership. This is essential not only for practical reasons (i.e., effective training is likely to encourage the organization to invest in more training in the future), but for ensuring that the team training continues to be effective. As discussed throughout this book, the support of organizational leadership is essential for the design, implementation, and maintenance of team training (see Guidelines 1, 5, 49, Principle 3).

Accordingly, presentation of results should focus on the outcomes of training that are most valuable to organizational leadership. Reaction and learning data are valuable, but behavior and results metrics are of most interest to leadership. It should be noted that organizational results data is similar to behavior metrics, in that it is of supreme interest to organizational clients, but is also very difficult to clearly link to training because of the plethora of confounding factors in effect at this level. Nonetheless, by collaborating with organizational leadership to identify the importance and value associated with different learning objectives, training developers and facilitators can garner support by clearly communicating the positive effects that training has on desirable, agreed-upon objectives.

---

## TIPS AND ADVICE

- Identify strengths and shortcomings of the team training program.
- Link performance diagnostics with learning objectives.
- Document trends in teamwork processes and outcomes that were observed in the training cycle.
- Specify the degree to which improvements in team performance can be linked to team training.
- Approximate the extent to which improved team performance enhanced organizational goals.
- Estimate whether the return on investment from team training justifies team training expenditures.
- Propose revisions, if necessary, to improve the effectiveness of team training.
- Ensure evaluation continuity by having a plan for employee turnover at both the participant and evaluation administration team levels.

Adapted from: Aguinis & Kraiger, 2009; Salas, Burke, Bowers, & Wilson, 2001; Weaver, Salas, & King, 2011.

---

## Notes

1  Brannick & Prince, 1997; Dickinson & McIntyre, 1997
2  Rosen, Salas, Silvestri, Wu, & Lazzara, 2008; Rosen et al., 2010
3  Aguinis & Kraiger, 2009; Salas et al., 2009
4  Brannick & Prince, 1997; Salas, Burke, & Fowlkes, 2006; Salas, Cannon-Bowers, & Smith-Jentsch, 2006
5  Hackman, 2003; Salas et al., 2009
6  Kraiger, Ford, & Salas, 1993
7  See also Principle 9.
8  Baker & Salas, 1997
9  Aguinis & Kraiger, 2009
10  Salas & Stagl, 2009

# References

Aguinis, H., & Kraiger, K. (2009). Benefits of training and development for individuals and teams, organizations, and society. *Annual Review of Psychology, 60,* 451–474.

Alliger, G. M., Tannenbaum, S. I., Bennet Jr. W., Traver, H., & Shotland, A. (1997). A meta-analysis of the relations among training criteria. *Personnel Psychology, 50*(2), 341–358.

Baker, D. P., & Salas, E. (1997). Principles for measuring teamwork: A summary and look toward the future. In M.T. Brannick, E. Salas, & C. Prince (Eds.), *Team performance assessment and measurement theory, methods, and applications* (pp. 331–335). Mahwah, NJ: Lawrence Erlbaum Associates.

Baldwin, T. P., & Ford, J. K. (1988). Transfer of training: A review and directions for future research. *Personnel Psychology, 41,* 63–105.

Brannick, M.T., & Prince, C. (1997). An overview of team performance measurement. In M.T. Brannick, E. Salas, & C. Prince (Eds.), *Team performance assessment and measurement: Theory, methods, and applications* (pp. 3–16). Mahwah, NJ: Lawrence Erlbaum Associates.

Dickinson, T.L., & McIntyre, R.M. (1997). A conceptual framework for teamwork measurement. In M.T. Brannick, E. Salas, & C. Prince (Eds.), *Team performance assessment and measurement: Theory, methods, and applications* (pp. 19–43). Mahwah, NJ: Lawrence Erlbaum Associates.

Dwyer, D. J., & Salas, E. (2000). Principles of performance measurement for ensuring aircrew training effectiveness. In H. F. O'Neil Jr. & D. H. Andrews (Eds.), *Aircrew training and assessment* (pp. 223–244). Mahwah, NJ: Lawrence Erlbaum Associates.

Fleiss, J. L., & Cohen, J. (1973). The equivalence of weighted kappa and the intraclass correlation coefficient as measures of reliability. *Educational and Psychological Measurement, 33,* 613–619.

Flin, R., & Martin, L. (2001). Behavioral markers for crew resource management: A review of current practice. *International Journal of Aviation Psychology, 11*(1), 95–118.

Ford, D.N., & Sterman, J.D. (1998). Expert knowledge elicitation to improve formal and mental models. *System Dynamics Review, 14,* 309–340.

Gregory, M.E., Feitosa, J., Driskell, T., Salas, E, & Vessey, W.B. (2013). Designing, delivering, and evaluating training in organizations: Principles that work. In E. Salas, S.I. Tannenbaum, D. Cohen, & G. Latham (Eds.), *Developing and enhancing teamwork in organizations: Evidence-based best practices and guidelines* (pp. 441–487). San Francisco, CA: Jossey-Bass.

Hackman, J. R. (2003). Learning more by crossing levels: Evidence from airplanes, hospitals, and orchestras. *Journal of Organizational Behavior, 24*(8), 905–922.

Kendall, D. L., & Salas, E. (2004). Measuring team performance: Review of current methods and consideration of future needs. In J.W. Ness, V. Tepe, D. Ritzer (Eds.), *The science and simulation of human performance* (pp. 307–326). Amsterdam, The Netherlands: Elsevier.

Kirkpatrick, D.L. (1994). *Evaluating training programs.* New York, NY: McGraw-Hill.

Klein, C. K., Sims, D. E., & Salas, E. (2006). Training evaluation. In W. Karwowski (Ed.), *International encyclopedia of ergonomics and human factors* (pp. 2434–2439). London, UK: CRC Press.

Kraiger, K., Ford, J. K., & Salas, E. (1993). Application of cognitive, skill-based, and affective theories of learning outcomes to new methods of training evaluation. *Journal of Applied Psychology, 78*(2), 311–328.

LaFrance, M. (1989). The quality of expertise: Implications of expert-novice differences for knowledge acquisition. *ACM SIGART Bulletin, 108,* 6–14.

Littrell, L. N., & Salas, E. (2005). A review of cross-cultural training: Best practices, guidelines, and research needs. *Human Resource Development Review, 4*(3), 305–334.

Mack, N., Woodsong, C., MacQueen, K. M., Guest, G., & Namey, E. (2011). *Qualitative research methods: A data collector's field guide*. Research Triangle Park, NC: Family Health International.

O'Byrne, K., Clark, R. E., & Malakuti, R. (1997). Expert and novice performance: Implications for clinical training. *Educational Psychology Review, 9*(4), 321–332.

Paris, C. R., Salas, E., & Cannon-Bowers, J. A., (2000). Teamwork in multi-person systems: A review and analysis. *Ergonomics, 43*(8), 1052–1075.

Patton, M. Q. (2008). *Utilization-focus evaluation*. Thousand Oaks, CA: Sage.

Rosen, M. A., Salas, E., Silvestri, S., Wu, T., & Lazzara, E. H. (2008). A measurement tool for simulation-based training in emergency medicine: The simulation module for assessment of resident targeted event responses (SMARTER) approach. *Simulation in Healthcare, 3*(3), 170–179.

Rosen, M. A., Salas, E., Wilson, K. A., King, H. B., Salisbury, M., … Birnbach, D. J. (2008). Measuring team performance in simulation-based training: Adopting best practices for health care. *Simulation in Healthcare, 3*(1), 33–41.

Rosen, M. A., Weaver, S. J., Lazzara, E. H., Salas, E., Wu, T., Silvestri, S, … King, H. (2010). Tools for evaluating team performance in simulation-based training. *Journal of Emergencies, Trauma, and Shock, 3*(4), 353–359.

Russ-Eft, D., & Preskill, H. (2009). *Evaluation in organizations*. New York, NY: Basic Books.

Ryder, J. M., & Redding, R. E. (1993). Integrating cognitive task analysis into instructional systems development. *Educational Technology Research and Development, 41*, 75–96.

Salas E. (2006). Team training. In W. Karwowski (Ed.), *International encyclopedia of ergonomics and human factors* (pp. 2394–2397). London, UK: Taylor & Francis.

Salas, E., Burke, C.S., Bowers, C.A., & Wilson, K.A. (2001). Team training in the skies: Does crew resource management (CRM) training work? *Human Factors, 43*(4), 641–674.

Salas, E., Burke, C.S., & Cannon-Bowers, J.A. (2002). What we know about designing and delivering team training: Tips and guidelines. In K. Kraiger (Ed.), *Creating, implementing, and managing effective training and development: State-of-the-art lessons for practice* (pp. 234–259). San Francisco, CA: Jossey-Bass.

Salas, E., Burke, C. S., & Fowlkes, J. E. (2006). Measuring team performance "in the wild": Challenges and tips. In W. Bennett, C. Lance, & D. Woehr (Eds.), *Performance measurement: Current perspectives and future challenges* (pp. 245–272). Mahwah, NJ: Lawrence Erlbaum Associates.

Salas, E., & Cannon-Bowers, J.A. (2000). The anatomy of team training. In S. Tobias & J. D. Fletcher (Eds.), *Training and retraining: A handbook for business, industry, and government* (pp. 312–335). New York, NY: Macmillan Reference.

Salas, E., Cannon-Bowers, J.A., & Smith-Jentsch, K.A. (2006). Principles and strategies for team training. In W. Karwowski (Ed.), *International Encyclopedia of Ergonomics and Human Factors* (pp. 2245–2248). Boca Raton, FL: CRC Press.

Salas, E., & Rosen, M. A. (2009). Performance assessment. In D. Schmorrow, J. Cohn, & D. Nicholson (Eds.), *The PSI handbook of virtual environments for training and education: Developments for the military and beyond* (pp. 227–235). Westport, CT: Praeger Security International.

Salas, E., Rosen, M. A., Burke, C. S., Nicholson, D., & Howse, W. R. (2007). Markers for enhancing team cognition in complex environments: The power of team performance diagnosis. *Aviation, Space, and Environmental Medicine, 78*(5), B77–B85.

Salas, E., Rosen, M. A., Weaver, S. J., Held, J. D., & Weissmuller, J. J. (2009). Guidelines for performance measurement in simulation-based training. *Ergonomics in Design, 17*(4), 12–18.

Salas, E., Shuffler, M. L., Thayer, A. L., Bedwell, W. L., & Lazzara, E. H. (in press). Understanding and diagnosing teamwork in organizations: A scientifically-based practical guide. *Human Resource Management.*

Salas, E., & Stagl, K. C. (2009). Design training systematically and follow the science of training. In E. A. Locke (Ed.), *Handbook of principles of organizational behavior: Indispensable knowledge for evidence-based management* (pp. 59–84). West Sussex, UK: Wiley and Sons.

Salas, E., Wilson, K. A., Priest, H. A., & Guthrie, J. W. (2006). Design, delivery, and evaluation of training systems. In G. Salvend (Ed.), *Handbook of human factors and ergonomics* (pp. 472–512). Hoboken, NJ: John Wiley & Sons.

Shadish W. R., Cook, T. D., & Campbell, D. T. (2002). *Experimental and quasi-experimental designs for generalized causal inference.* Boston, MA: Houghton Mifflin Company.

Shapiro, M. J., Gardner, R., Godwin, S. A., Jay, G. D., Lindquist, D. G., Salisbury, M. L., & Salas, E. (2008). Defining team performance for simulation-based training: Methodology, metrics, and opportunities for emergency medicine. *Academic Emergency Medicine, 15*(11), 1088–1097.

Weaver, S.J., Salas, E., & King, H.B. (2011). Twelve best practices for team training evaluation in health care. *The Joint Commission Journal on Quality and Patient Safety, 37*(8), 341–349.

# 6

## PILLAR 5

## Create a System for Enduring and Sustaining Teamwork Behaviors in Organizations

**Is completing team training and initial evaluations the end of the story?** The completion of the formal training and evaluation periods should not signal the end of the broader team training process. To reap the benefits of

> Training Transfer: The degree to which learning that results from training is applied, generalized, and maintained on the job.

the various steps that have been taken up to this point, efforts should be made to ensure that trained teamwork behaviors are enduring and sustainable over time. This is necessary because team training itself is not sufficient for ensuring that meaningful changes in teamwork observed in the training environment actually occur within the organizational context, particularly as time progresses. Indeed, researchers and practitioners have long lamented the "transfer problem" (Michalak, 1985), which refers to the observation that only about 10% of training expenditures are transferred to the job (Georgenson, 1982). **Training transfer** refers to the degree to which learning that results from training is applied, generalized, and maintained on the job (Ford & Weissbein, 1997; Goldstein & Ford, 2002). In the context of team training, transfer means that after training, teams use trained teamwork and taskwork behaviors in the job setting (i.e., application), apply them to a variety of situations, not just the one(s) encountered during training (i.e., generalization), and continue to use them appropriately long after the training has been completed (i.e., maintenance).

Fortunately, research shows that a variety of actions can be taken to help ensure that teamwork behaviors are transferred and sustained over time (Blume, Ford, Baldwin, & Huang, 2010; Burke & Hutchins, 2007; Grossman & Salas, 2011). For example, a supportive climate can make a world of difference in determining whether or not learners utilize teamwork behaviors appropriately in their everyday work. Additionally, a set of procedures for continually evaluating and improving team training can help ensure that both old and new employees receive training that is high quality, consistent, and relevant to broader organizational goals. In the following set of principles, guidelines, and tips/advice, we provide specific information about why and how organizations can establish a system for ensuring that teamwork behaviors are endured and sustained over time.

## Principle 12: Establish Mechanisms for the Continued Assessment and Improvement of Team Training

If one team training evaluation showed that team training was effective, it does not necessarily mean that all future iterations of the training will also be effective. As discussed throughout, characteristics of the organizational environment, the learners, and the work itself, among other things, can all influence the degree to which a particular training approach is successful (Baldwin & Ford, 1988). Because these things tend to change over time (e.g., new personnel are hired, primary tasks change to meet market demands), the efficacy of team training may also change, even if the content does not. It is therefore important for organizations to continue to assess team training well beyond the initial evaluation effort. Additionally, efforts should be made to update and improve the content of the existing training program (O'Connor, Han, & Salas, 2010), both in response to the results of the training evaluation, and as new research, technology, and other resources become available. The following guidelines and tips provide insight about how organizations can establish mechanisms to help ensure that their team training remains effective as time goes on and organizational changes take place.

### Guideline 41: Update Team Training in Response to Team Training Evaluation Results[1]

The results of the team training evaluation will provide valuable information about what is and what is not working (see Pillar 4); accordingly, team training should be updated and improved upon to reflect the evaluation results, as necessary (Grossman & Salas, 2013; Salas, Wilson, Burke, & Priest, 2006). For example, if the evaluation reveals that one of the teamwork KSAs was not sufficiently trained, team training will need to be revised to better target that KSA in future training administrations. Likewise, if there is a component of the training that learners had negative reactions to, such as a particular trainer or computer program, these issues should be addressed before team training is administered again. Negative attitudes toward training can spread among both old and new learners, and can reduce the likelihood that learners will learn from and apply future team training (Grossman & Salas, 2011).

When implementing changes, however, it is important to keep the broader team training system in mind. For example, switching from a lower to higher form of technology for delivering teamwork demonstrations can introduce new costs, require new resources, and influence learners in different ways, impacting various components of the team training process. Additionally, organizational stakeholders need to be made aware of changes and why they are being implemented to help ensure that they continue to advocate for team training as it evolves and improves (Weaver, Salas, & King, 2011).

---

## TIPS AND ADVICE

- Implement changes suggested by the results of the team training evaluation.
- Consider making changes to both the selection procedures as well as the training itself.
- Update and improve the content of the existing training program.
- Ensure that stakeholders are clearly aware of the benefits of implementing the changes.
- Consider how changes might impact the broader training system.

Adapted from: Weaver et al., 2011.

---

### Guideline 42: Establish and Implement a Plan to Continue Team Training and Monitor Its Impact over Time[2]

Research suggests that team training should be an ongoing process (Salas & Priest, 2005; Salas, Weaver, & Wildman, 2009). This means that once the initial team training has been administered, the job is not over. Indeed, without some form of refresher or additional training,

> Without refresher training, 92% of what is learned during training will decay within one year of training.

approximately 92% of what is learned during training is likely to decay within only a year after training (Arthur, Bennet, Stanush, & McNelly, 1998). A plan should therefore be implemented not only for continuing team training, but also for evaluating its effectiveness over time (Shuffler, Salas, & Xavier, 2010; Oser, Salas, Merket, & Bowers, 2001).

Future team training should focus both on providing additional learning opportunities to those who have undergone initial training, and on integrating new personnel who will need to learn teamwork KSAs for the first time (Weaver, Salas, & Rosen, 2009). Establishing a system for doing these things can help ensure that such learning opportunities do not "fall through the cracks," leading to an eventual decline in quality teamwork behaviors. This evaluation system should assess trained and untrained individuals and teams on the trained teamwork competencies, monitor skill decay, and identify indicators that refresher training is needed again. Because continuously assessing team training can become cumbersome, it is important to establish procedures that are efficient and that collect meaningful information. For example, performance measures should be automated whenever possible (Salas, Rosen, Weaver, Held, & Weissmuller, 2009), or, at the least, streamlined by establishing a detailed and consistent system for collecting and analyzing them. Additionally, to be of most use, the system should be designed to evaluate performance and to facilitate specific feedback for both individuals and teams (Shuffler et al., 2010).

---

## TIPS AND ADVICE

- Collect longitudinal data at the individual, team, and organizational levels to assess the effects of training over time.
- Automate as much of the performance measurement collection and analysis as possible.
- Ensure that team performance measurement systems can distinguish between individual and team level deficiencies.
- Design team performance measurement systems to produce assessments that can be used to deliver specific performance feedback.
- Have a plan for integrating new members into the team training cycle and execute it.
- Repeat training periodically to prevent skill decay over time.

Adapted from: Salas, Rosen, et al., 2009.

---

### Guideline 43: Continue to Assess Team Training Needs in Light of Organizational Goals

> Monitor training effectiveness in light of changing organizational goals, as they will influence training effectiveness indices.

Organizational practices and goals can change over time, and these changes can influence the extent to which team training is still appropriate in its original form. For example, if an organization changes from a hierarchical to a team-based structure, this could mean that *everyone* in the organization will need team training, not just the select group of learners who may have initially received it. A change in organizational strategy could also necessitate different kinds of team training, as different strategies may require different kinds of teams or teamwork competencies. For example, shifting the organizational strategy from emphasizing cost minimization to quality, creativity, and innovation may mean that teamwork behaviors that facilitate creativity—such as honesty, trust, and shared positive attitude toward learning—become more important learning objectives for future team training (Drach-Zahavy & Somech, 2001; Edmondson & Nembhard, 2009). Similarly, as organizational goals change, it is possible that team training may no longer be the ideal solution for meeting organizational needs. It is important to keep this in mind because performance data may make it appear that team training is no longer effective, when in fact, it simply is no longer relevant to reaching new performance goals. Therefore, many of the actions described in Pillar 1 may need to be reproduced if organizational changes are substantial.

---

## TIPS AND ADVICE

- Remain aware of changes in organizational practices that may influence the long-term maintenance of training.
- Assess the trained teamwork behaviors and organizational goals regularly.
- Assess the degree to which teamwork behaviors are still relevant to organizational goals and adjust team training accordingly.

Adapted from: Kozlowski, Brown, Weissbein, Cannon-Bowers, & Salas, 2000.

---

## Principle 13: Provide Opportunities to Foster Continual Team Improvement

Even if individuals *learn* from training, there is no guarantee that they will put that learning to use in the work environment, especially as time progresses (Grossman & Salas, 2011). Steps should therefore be taken to facilitate transfer, the application of trained knowledge and skills to the job (Goldstein & Ford, 2002). While several things can be done before training even begins (see Pillar 2), there are a variety of opportunities to further facilitate learning and transfer once the official training has been completed. These mainly involve administering feedback and facilitating discussion relevant to the trained teamwork behaviors, providing learners with opportunities to use what they have learned within the work environment, and supplying support, of various kinds, that is necessary for learners to be able to successfully perform. Ultimately, the training facilitator should take steps to ensure that: (1) learners understand that trained teamwork competencies are important in the workplace (i.e., not just in the training setting), (2) learners' attention is consistently focused on executing trained team competencies, and (3) organizational leadership continually reinforces this importance by offering opportunities for refresher training and continuous improvement.

### Guideline 44: Conduct Team Training Debriefings Organized Around Key Events and Learning Objectives[3]

Absent clear feedback, learners may not have an accurate idea of how well they performed during team training. Similarly, without consistent debriefings focused on trained team competencies, learners will be unaware of the degree to which they are effectively using teamwork behaviors upon returning to the work environment. This is problematic because in order for learners to address issues that may arise in their teamwork behaviors after training, they first need to know that there are problems to address. Additionally, learners may end up acquiring incorrect or incomplete information from team training that can have negative consequences when it is applied to the workplace. For example, learners in a conflict management team training program may assume that a step-by-step conflict resolution procedure is necessary in every single situation, whereas it may only be needed in very specific situations. Once team training is complete, it is therefore important to utilize debriefs—simple, yet powerful tools that are designed to reinforce previous learning material, and to provide opportunities for additional learning to take place (Salas, Tannenbaum, Kraiger, & Smith-Jentsch, 2012).

> Debriefs allow team members to reflect on recent experiences, identify areas of strengths and weaknesses, and voice questions and concerns regarding learning material or recent team performance.

Debriefs focused on trained teamwork behaviors can be used immediately after training or periodically within the work environment. During a debrief, a team leader or person external to the team facilitates a formal discussion where team members reflect on recent experiences, identify areas of strengths and weaknesses, and voice questions or concerns regarding learning material or recent team performance. Teams that utilize debriefs effectively have been shown to perform better than teams that do not (Smith-Jentsch, Cannon-Bowers, Tannenbaum, & Salas, 2008; Tannenbaum, Smith-Jentsch, & Behson, 1998), suggesting that they are a valuable tool for ensuring that trained teamwork behaviors are maintained appropriately over time. If not conducted appropriately, however, teams will not reap the maximum benefit of team debriefing exercises. Research on team debriefs suggest a few best practices. First, the role of teamwork behaviors in the team's performance needs to be clearly explained (Salas et al., 2008). This is to enable the team to know what team competencies they need to focus on, and why. Second, feedback needs to be delivered constructively (Smith-Jentsch, Baker, Salas, & Cannon-Bowers, 2001) and respectfully; vague, destructive feedback will neither reinforce old learning nor facilitate new learning. Below, we provide a variety of tips that can help ensure that debriefs are effective.

---

**TIPS AND ADVICE**

- Describe specific teamwork interactions and processes that were involved in the team's performance.
- Focus on a few critical performance issues during the debriefing process.
- Identify lessons learned and areas for continued improvement to guide self-development efforts.
- Provide information about how team members can state their comments in a constructive manner.
- Guide self-correction by keeping the debriefing discussion focused and modeling effective feedback skills.
- Ensure that everyone has an opportunity to provide constructive feedback.
- Reserve input for times when trainees cannot generate input or when clarifications are required.
- Incorporate both individual- and team-level feedback.
- Discuss both positive and negative aspects of team performance during debriefs.
- Make sure that team members feel comfortable during debriefs.
- Record conclusions and goals set during the debrief to facilitate feedback during future debriefs.

Adapted from: Smith-Jentsch et al., 2008; Tannenbaum & Cerasoli, 2013.

---

### Guideline 45: Provide Opportunities for Trainees to Use Trained Teamwork Skills on the Job[4]

Not surprisingly, learners need to be given plenty of opportunities to practice and apply their new teamwork skills in the workplace if they are to effectively transfer them to the job (Burke & Hutchins, 2008). This may seem obvious, but often standardized procedures and work schedules do not allow the time for learners to utilize what they learned. Indeed, a lack of opportunities to use new skills on the job has been named one of the strongest barriers to successful transfer of training (Clarke, 2002). Trainees need opportunities to use new teamwork skills not only to *maintain* them over time, but also to apply them to a variety of situations, or to *generalize* them, both important components of training transfer (Ford & Weissbein, 1997). Following training, learners' workloads and, if necessary, tasks should therefore be modified to allow them to practice using trained teamwork behaviors in the context of their jobs (Clarke, 2002). To maximize effectiveness, the time between the team training and these practice opportunities should be as short as possible (Salas, Wilson, Priest, & Guthrie, 2006).

---

### TIPS AND ADVICE

- Minimize the time between team training and the opportunities for train-ees to use trained teamwork skills on the job.
- Allow for temporary shifts in workload to ensure that trainees have oppor-tunities to practice using new skills appropriately.
- Provide multiple practice opportunities to allow trainees to practice the trained knowledge and skills on multiple occasions.

Adapted from: Clarke, 2002; Salas, Wilson, Priest, et al., 2006.

---

### Guideline 46: Provide Feedback Regarding Trainees' Use of Trained Teamwork Skills on the Job[5]

**Good feedback is:**

*Specific about what the learner is doing right/wrong
*Timely
*Linked to learning objectives
*Provided to both individuals and the whole team

For learners to be able to sustain desired teamwork behaviors in the future, they need to know what they are doing right, and what they are doing wrong at the current time. This is where feedback becomes critical. Feedback in this case involves a supervisor or team leader providing information to learners about some aspect of their performance of trained teamwork behaviors (Kluger & DeNisi, 1996). Because learners may be unclear on how to apply some of the training content to the workplace, missteps in executing trained team KSAs are to be expected. Feedback should therefore be provided frequently and as soon after team training as possible (Wildman, Salas, Priest, Lyons, & Carnegie, 2009). Additionally, to prevent a decline or misuse of teamwork behaviors, it should be provided often, and continuously, long after training is over (Salas, Wildman, & Piccolo, 2009).

However, feedback is not intrinsically helpful—it must be *good* feedback (Salas, Weaver, DiazGranados, Lyons, & King, 2009). Effective feedback is not only timely (as discussed above and in Guideline 24), but *diagnostic*, meaning that *specific* information about *why* a learner's performance is considered good or bad is provided to the learner (Salas, Wildman, & Piccolo, 2009; Weaver, Salas, King, &

DiazGranados, 2008; Wilson, Salas, & Lyons, 2008). This way, learners will know what exactly they need to change and what to keep doing the same in order to achieve desirable levels of teamwork behaviors. Additionally, care should be taken to ensure that feedback is *specific to* learners, but not *critical of* them (Coultas, Grossman, & Salas, 2012). Feedback that criticizes learners and threatens their positive perception of and feelings towards themselves will distract them from learning and improving, focusing their attention more on the negative feelings associated with critical feedback. To avoid this, feedback should be clearly related to the learning objectives clearly stated in team training (Salas, Oser, Cannon-Bowers, & Daskarolis, 2002), as well as broader indicators of performance (Salas et al., 2008), such as team productivity. Finally, as discussed in Guideline 44, respectful feedback (e.g., communicating care, avoiding public embarrassment) will also help the learner avoid being distracted by negative emotions and instead focus on learning and improving.

---

## TIPS AND ADVICE

- Shorten the delay between teamwork performance and feedback as much as possible.
- Provide feedback at both the individual and team level.
- Directly relate feedback to the learning objectives of the training.
- Ensure that feedback is diagnostic such that specific information is provided about what the trainee did right or wrong and how he/she can improve.
- Deliver feedback that is specific to the performance of the trainee, but not critical of the person.
- Support feedback with objective indicators of performance.
- Provide outcome feedback later and less frequently than process feedback.
- Provide remediation through additional targeted training when deficiencies are communicated.
- Ensure trainees are provided support back on the job site to apply new behaviors.

Adapted from: Kluger & DeNisi, 1996; Salas, Burke, & Cannon-Bowers, 2002; Tannenbaum & Cerasoli, 2013.

---

## Principle 14: Motivate and Facilitate the Long-Term Transfer and Sustainment of Teamwork Behaviors[6]

Learners are more likely to transfer training content to the job when they are motivated to do so, and when they perceive training as valuable and instrumental in achieving outcomes they care about (Grossman & Salas, 2011). For example, if learners believe that attempting to resolve conflict will only invite a backlash from others, or if they believe that helping others will not be recognized and will simply be a drain on already limited time resources, they will be unlikely to engage in these behaviors—regardless of how effective the training may have appeared to be in the training setting. Efforts should therefore be made to establish a climate in the workplace that encourages, rewards, and supports the continued use of trained teamwork behaviors long after team training is complete (Salas et al., 2012). A reward system should be implemented to reinforce learners' appropriate use of trained teamwork behaviors on the job. Part of this reward system would necessarily involve establishing goals for the performance of trained team competencies and behaviors. Establishing these goals and implementing rewards at the team- as opposed to the individual-level is especially important for creating a focus on teamwork and communicating that the organization values teamwork behaviors (Cannon-Bowers, Salas, & Milham, 2000).

Additionally, to help learners sustain teamwork behaviors over time, organizational leadership should make efforts to establish open lines of communication between themselves and learners (Wildman et al., 2009). Organizational leaders should continually communicate the importance of trained team competencies—both through explicit messages and implicit modeling of desirable behaviors. Aspects of climate, culture, or structure that may complicate the execution of trained team competencies—such as unsupportive or negative employees, excessive workload, or even workspace design—should also be addressed. Excessive workload may make it infeasible or impossible for learners to attempt to apply their training to the job. Providing appropriate resources that facilitate the use and maintenance of teamwork behaviors can be one way to minimize effort associated with either the actual job or practicing trained behaviors. Job aids, for example, are tools designed to assist with performance; these can be implemented to help reduce the amount of effort necessary to utilize trained teamwork behaviors on the job (Salas, Wilson, Priest, et al., 2006), as described further below (Guideline 51).

### Guideline 47: Support a Constant Flow of Communication by Encouraging Trainees to Voice Questions or Comments Regarding the Appropriate Use of Trained Teamwork Skills

Learners may encounter issues or questions as they begin to utilize trained teamwork behaviors within the work environment. Addressing these issues can not only prevent learners from becoming discouraged when attempting to use teamwork behaviors, but it can help correct deficient or misappropriated teamwork behaviors. Organizational leaders should establish open lines of communication not only to address learners' comments and concerns, but also to allow learners to use each other as resources for reinforcing and refining teamwork behaviors. These communication lines should be targeted, however. Rather than simply encouraging the use of an open comment box, upward feedback (i.e., learners communicating with leaders) should follow the same rules as any other feedback. That is, it should be specific, constructive, and directed

> Communication systems can help improve future training and maintain its long-term effectiveness—provided communication is honest, relevant, and constructive.

at team/task objectives (see Guideline 44). Part of this specificity should also be tied to the learning objectives. Learners should be encouraged to ask questions, provide feedback, and report difficulties associated particularly with their attempts to apply trained team KSAs to the workplace. Peer-to-peer or lateral communication can also be a helpful way to encourage the continued used of trained team KSAs. Learners can ask questions of other learners who seem to be effectively integrating new behaviors into their everyday work life, enabling continual learning. Lateral communication can also function as a repository for sharing positive stories of effective teamwork—this may help learners to maintain their motivation to engage in effective team behaviors. However, to be of use, both upward and lateral communication systems need to be managed appropriately—concerns should be addressed in a timely, consistent manner, and it should be made clear to learners that questions and errors they voice regarding teamwork behaviors will not have punitive consequences (Wilson-Donnelly, Priest, Salas, & Burke, 2005).

---

## TIPS AND ADVICE

- Establish a system through which trainees can voice their comments and concerns on a regular basis without punitive consequences.
- Ensure that comments and concerns are addressed, and do so in a timely manner.
- Create a system through which trainees can use each other as resources.
- Encourage non-punitive discussion and documentation of errors.

Adapted from: Salas et al., 2012; Wilson-Donnelly et al., 2005.

---

### Guideline 48: Establish a Climate in the Workplace That Encourages the Use of Trained Teamwork Skills[7]

No matter how good team training is, if the climate in the workplace does not encourage the use of trained teamwork behaviors, it is unlikely that learners will

> A positive transfer climate encourages the use of trained teamwork behaviors in the work environment through cues, rewards, support, and feedback.

use them after training is complete (Blume et al., 2010; Colquitt et al., 2000). More specifically, it is important to develop a positive transfer climate, a situation in the organization that either encourages or discourages the use of learned knowledge and skills (Rouiller & Goldstein, 1993). A positive transfer climate can be established through things like cues or triggers that remind learners to use teamwork behaviors, rewards for correctly executing team behaviors, consequences or remediation for the incorrect use of teamwork behaviors, and providing support through feedback, job aids, and other resources (Grossman & Salas, 2011). For example, if organizational leaders discuss the importance of teamwork, conduct performance appraisals on the basis of teamwork behaviors, and offer incentives and rewards for the appropriate use of teamwork behaviors, it sends a clear message that teamwork is valued by the organization and should be utilized by the learners. In contrast, if they do none of these things, or worse, send negative messages about teamwork, learners will be hesitant to apply what they learned from team training to their jobs.

A comprehensive approach is necessary to communicate and create a positive transfer climate. That is, simply *saying* that teamwork is important is not enough—actions and organizational practices need to *show* that it is important, by implementing the things described above, for example (Burke, Salas, Wilson-Donnelly, & Priest, 2004). Additionally, it is especially critical to ensure that learners' performance is evaluated based on their use of trained teamwork behaviors (Salas, Weaver, & Wildman, 2009; Weaver et al., 2008; Weaver et al., 2009). If learners know that their use of teamwork behaviors will never be assessed or related to outcomes that they care about, they will be less motivated to use them. All of these things help create a positive transfer climate that will make it far more likely that trained teamwork behaviors will be applied and maintained in the work environment (Salas, Wilson, Priest, et al., 2006; Salas, Wilson-Donnelly, Sims, Burke, & Priest, 2007; Weaver et al., 2011).

---

## TIPS AND ADVICE

- Disseminate findings from your training evaluation to stakeholders, managers, and trainees.
- Ensure everyone has a clear understanding of the implications of evaluation findings.
- Share success stories throughout the organization.

- Establish environmental signals that indicate that the trained KSAs and performance evaluations are valued by the organization.
- Ensure that latent organizational messages about the importance of team training match those that are spoken.
- Encourage all personnel to support trainees' use of trained teamwork skills on the job.
- Track the team's actions, events, progress, and products.
- Regularly review team communications for interpersonal conflicts and performance concerns—intervene early.
- Communicate with the team often and facilitate the regular exchange of situation updates.
- Promote an organizational climate that encourages continuous learning.
- Model the desired team behaviors—members see, members do!

Adapted from: Grossman & Salas, 2011; Salas, Rosen, et al., 2009.

## Guideline 49: Continue to Encourage Leadership and Management to Reinforce and Model Desired Teamwork Behaviors[8]

Organizational leadership should continue to champion and reinforce trained teamwork behaviors long after training is over—this will help establish the positive transfer climate described above in Guideline 48 (Grossman & Salas, 2011). However, leaders may not be aware of the signals they are sending or how to communicate the signals that they want to convey. Supervisors and team leaders should therefore be trained how to establish and maintain a climate in the workplace that supports the development and continued use of teamwork behaviors on the job (Smith-Jentsch et al., 2001). Training leaders to communicate a positive teamwork climate constitutes something of team training as well; accordingly, the pillars, principles, guidelines, and tips discussed in reference to broader team training are relevant for leader-specific training as well. For example, leaders' current KSAs for creating the correct climate should be assessed. If leader training is deemed necessary, it should be designed systematically and measured consistently to assess effectiveness. Additionally, upper management or trainers should periodically ensure that these leaders are consistently modeling teamwork behaviors (Wildman, Salas et al., 2009), and communicating the value of using them to their subordinates (Salas & Cannon-Bowers, 2000). Equipping leaders with the tools they need to utilize and encourage teamwork behaviors appropriately can go a long way in seeing that the trained team competencies and KSAs are applied and maintained in the workplace.

---

**TIPS AND ADVICE**

- Provide supplemental training to team leaders in team performance concepts (beyond that provided to team members).
- Further educate team leaders on the art and science of leading team debriefs.
- Train supervisors and team leaders to create and maintain a climate that reinforces the development and use of effective team competencies on the job.
- Ensure that leadership models the desired team behaviors.
- Encourage leadership to emphasize the value of newly acquired teamwork KSAs.

Adapted from: Smith-Jentsch et al., 2001; Tannenbaum et al., 1998; Wildman et al., 2009.

---

## Guideline 50: Implement Rewards and Consequences for the Use/Lack of Use of Trained Teamwork Skills

> Providing rewards for using trained teamwork behaviors is only useful if learners care about those rewards.

As a part of creating a positive climate for transfer, it is important for the organization to establish a formal system for providing rewards and consequences for the appropriate use, or lack of use, of trained teamwork behaviors (Grossman & Salas, 2011). As discussed in Guideline 48, learners' performance of teamwork behaviors should be formally evaluated, and the results of these evaluations should be related to outcomes (e.g., incentives, consequences) that learners care about (Salas, Weaver, & Wildman, 2009; Weaver et al., 2008; Weaver et al., 2009). For example, if organizational leaders plan to reward strong use of teamwork behaviors by providing public recognition, they should first determine if recognition is something that is valued by the learners, or if another type of reward, such as monetary bonuses, would be more motivating. Similarly, if the consequences put in place for failing to use teamwork behaviors are not perceived as undesirable, they may not be sufficiently motivating because learners may prefer simply risking these consequences over putting forth the effort to engage in teamwork behaviors. It should be noted that positive reinforcement such as monetary rewards or recognition are typically seen as more effective than blatant punishment, as learners may come to resent feeling "forced" or "threatened" into engaging in certain behaviors.

One particularly effective approach for implementing rewards and consequences is the process of goal-setting, where specific, yet difficult goals for both the near and distant future are established for the use of trained KSAs (Locke & Latham, 2002). Goal-setting can increase the use of teamwork behaviors by directing learners' attention, motivating action, increasing persistence, and essentially prompting learners to use them. To be especially effective in this context, goals should be established for both teams as a whole, and individual members of the teams, and should be designed to be flexible so that the team grows with each new goal that is achieved (Weaver et al., 2009). When goals for using teamwork behaviors are linked to rewards and consequences of value, they can be powerful tools for facilitating their application and maintenance.

---

## TIPS AND ADVICE

- Provide incentives for transferring desired teamwork behaviors to the workplace.
- Include teamwork competencies in formal performance evaluations.
- Measure typical performance often (i.e., performance outside of formal evaluation periods).
- Ensure that trainees are aware of the system of rewards and consequences that is put in place.
- Implement rewards and consequences that are valued and/or meaningful to the trainees.
- Establish specific, difficult goals for the team and provide rewards or consequences when such goals are/are not achieved.
- Create goals the team can grow with—build hierarchically aligned goals with flexibility at both the individual and the team levels.

Adapted from: Locke & Latham, 2002; Salas, Weaver, & Wildman, 2009; Stevens & Campion, 1994; Weaver et al., 2008; Weaver et al., 2009.

---

## Guideline 51: Supply Trainees with the Resources They Need to Maintain Trained Teamwork Skills over Time

Beyond the support that a positive transfer climate can provide, learners may need additional support in the form of resources that help them sustain trained teamwork behaviors over time. Maintaining trained KSAs can become difficult in the everyday workplace because learners often need to juggle competing goals typical of taskwork performance with new and sometimes resource-intensive teamwork behaviors. This is difficult in itself, but to further complicate matters, the job conditions that may have necessitated team training in the first place will likely still be there after team training. For example, if hectic or poorly aligned work schedules contributed to poor communication behaviors prior to training—and assuming that team training needs analysis did not identify this as the primary cause of poor communication—learners will need to exert extra effort to practice trained KSAs in spite of the scheduling complications. Consider also a team that had trouble managing conflict due to the stresses of dealing with problematic customers; learners within these teams would need to practice trained conflict management KSAs while still interacting with the source of stress.

> Providing training reference materials (job aids) or even simple reminders to use trained team KSAs will go a long way towards facilitating the long-term transfer of training.

Organizations can facilitate the transfer of training by providing resources that can encourage or facilitate the use of trained team competencies. **Job aids**, for example, are tools that are designed to assist with performance, and can be implemented to help reduce the amount of effort that is necessary for learners to utilize trained behaviors (Salas, Wilson, Priest, et al., 2006). Job aids help by providing important instructions and other references materials, in turn reducing the mental workload that is required to apply trained KSAs to the work environment. Cues or prompts can also be implemented simply to help remind learners to continue to engage in trained KSAs. In cognitively taxing environments, it may be difficult or unreasonable to assume that learners will keep trained KSAs at the forefront of their thinking, while simultaneously addressing normal task demands. Reminding learners to engage in teamwork behaviors can be a welcome resource to facilitate the continual transfer of training. Finally, as mentioned throughout, team training is not a one-time thing—refresher training should be provided periodically (Salas & Priest, 2005; Salas, Weaver, & Wildman, 2009) to help prevent a natural decline in teamwork knowledge and skills. Because learners' use of teamwork behaviors should be regularly monitored, procedures should be established for preventing relapse and addressing performance deficiencies in between team training sessions (Salas & Cannon-Bowers, 2000). For example, additional coaching and modeling of teamwork behaviors by supervisors and team leaders can help reinforce learning material.

## TIPS AND ADVICE

- Create job aids in order to reduce the mental workload required to apply new skills to the workplace.
- Provide opportunities for refresher team training and provide training to new employees.
- Conduct regular debriefs to review proper and improper use of trained teamwork skills.

- Implement relapse prevention procedures to ensure that teamwork behaviors are maintained.
- Establish a program of ongoing training.

Adapted from: Gregory, Feitosa, Driskell, & Salas, 2013; Salas & Priest, 2005; Salas, Wilson, Priest, et al., 2006; Salas, Weaver, & Wildman, 2009.

## Notes

1  Grossman & Salas, 2013
2  Goldstein & Ford, 2002
3  Tannnenbaum & Cerasoli, 2013
4  Burke & Hutchins, 2007; Clarke, 2002
5  Kluger & DeNisi, 1996
6  Beier & Kanfer, 2010
7  Blume et al., 2010; Colquitt, LePine, & Noe, 2000
8  Bunch, 2007; Kozlowski et al., 2000; Salas & Cannon-Bowers, 2000; Wildman et al., 2009

## References

Arthur, W., Bennett, W., Stanush, P. L., & McNelly, T. L. (1998). Factors that influence skill decay and retention: A quantitative review and analysis. *Human Performance, 11*(1), 57–101.

Baldwin, T. T., & Ford, J. K. (1988). Transfer of training: A review and directions for future research. *Personnel Psychology, 41*(1), 63–105.

Beier, M.E., & Kanfer, R. (2010). Motivation in training and development: A phase perspective. In E. Salas & S.W.J. Kozlowski (Eds.), *Learning, training, and development in organizations* (pp. 65–98). New York, NY: Taylor & Francis Group.

Blume, B. D., Ford, J. K., Baldwin, T. T., & Huang, J. L. (2010). Transfer of training: A meta-analytic review. *Journal of Management, 36*(4), 1065–1105.

Bunch, K. J. (2007). Training failure as a consequence of organizational culture. *Human Resource Development Review, 6*(2), 152–163.

Burke, C. S., Salas, E., Wilson-Donnelly, K., & Priest, H. (2004). How to turn a team of experts into an expert medical team: Guidance from the aviation and military communities. *Quality and Safety in Health Care, 13*(1), i96–i104.

Burke, L. A., & Hutchins, H. M. (2007). Training transfer: An integrative literature review. *Human Resource Development Review, 6*(3), 263–296.

Burke, L. A., & Hutchins, H. M. (2008). A study of best practices in training transfer and proposed model of transfer. *Human Resource Development Quarterly, 19*(2), 107–128.

Cannon-Bowers, J., Salas, E., & Milham, L. (2000). The transfer of team training: Propositions and guidelines. *Managing and Changing Learning Transfer Systems in Organizations. Advances in Developing Human Resources, 8*, 63–74.

Clarke, N. (2002). Job/Work environment factors influencing training effectiveness within a human service agency: Some indicative support for Baldwin and Ford's transfer climate construct. *International Journal of Training and Development, 6*(3), 146–162.

Colquitt, J. A., LePine, J. A., & Noe, R. A. (2000). Toward an integrative theory of training motivation: A meta-analytic path analysis of 20 years of research. *Journal of Applied Psychology, 85*(5), 678–707.

Coultas, C. W., Grossman, R., & Salas, E. (2012). Design, delivery, evaluation, and transfer of training systems. In G. Salvendy (Ed.), *Handbook of human factors and ergonomics* (4th ed., pp. 490–522). Hoboken, NJ: John Wiley & Sons.

Drach-Zahavy, A., & Somech, A. (2001). Understanding team innovation: The role of team processes and structures. *Group Dynamics: Theory, Research and Practice, 5*(2), 111–123.

Edmondson, A. C., & Nembhard, I. M. (2009). Product development and learning in project teams: The challenges are the benefits. *Journal of Product Innovation Management, 26*(2), 123–138.

Ford, J. K., & Weissbein, D. (1997). Transfer of training: An updated review. *Performance Improvement Quarterly, 10*(2), 22–41.

Georgenson, D. L. (1982). The problem of transfer calls for partnership. *Training and Development Journal, 36*(10), 75–78.

Goldstein, I. L., & Ford, J. K. (2002). *Training in organizations* (4th ed.). Belmont, CA: Wadsworth Thompson Learning.

Gregory, M. E., Feitosa, J., Driskell, T., & Salas, E. (2013). Designing, delivering, and evaluating training in organizations: Principles that work. In E. Salas, S. I. Tannenbaum, D. Cohen, & G. Latham (Eds.), *Developing and enhancing teamwork in organizations: Evidence-based best practices and guidelines* (pp. 441–487). San Francisco, CA: Jossey-Bass.

Grossman, R., & Salas, E. (2011). The transfer of training: What really matters. *International Journal of Training and Development, 15*(2), 103–120.

Grossman, R., & Salas, E. (2013). Instructional features for training military teams in virtual environments. In C. Best, G. Galanis, J. Kerry, & R. Sottilare (Eds.), *Fundamental issues in defense training and simulation* (pp. 115–124). Burlington, VT: Ashgate Publishing Company.

Kluger, A. N., & DeNisi, A. (1996). The effects of feedback interventions on performance: A historical review, a meta-analysis, and a preliminary feedback intervention theory. *Psychological Bulletin, 119*(2), 254–284.

Kozlowski, S. W. J., Brown, K. G., Weissbein, D. A., Cannon-Bowers, J. A., & Salas, E. (2000). A multilevel approach to training effectiveness: Enhancing horizontal and vertical transfer. In K. J. Klein & S. W. J. Kozlowski (Eds.), *Multilevel theory, research, and methods in organizations: Foundations, extensions, and new directions* (pp. 157–210). San Francisco, CA: Jossey-Bass.

Locke, E. A., & Latham, G. P. (2002). Building a practically useful theory of goal setting and task motivation: A 35-year odyssey. *American Psychology, 57*(9), 705–717.

Michalak, D. F. (1985). The neglected half of training. *Training and Development Journal, 35*(5), 22–28.

O'Connor, P. E., Han, R. G., & Salas, E. (2010). The U.S. Navy's crew resource management program: The past, present, and recommendations for the future. In P. O'Connor & J. Cohn (Eds.), *Human performance enhancement in high-risk environments* (pp. 91–105). Santa Barbara, CA: Greenwood Publishing Group.

Oser, R. L., Salas, E., Merket, D. C., & Bowers, C. A. (2001). Applying resource management training in naval aviation: A methodology and lessons learned. In E. Salas, C. A. Bowers, & E. Edens (Eds.), *Improving teamwork in organizations: Applications of resource management training* (pp. 283–301). Mahwah, NJ: Lawrence Erlbaum Associates.

Rouiller, J. Z., & Goldstein, I. L. (1993). The relationship between organizational transfer climate and positive transfer of training. *Human Resources Development Quarterly, 4*(4), 377–390.

Salas, E., Burke, C. S., & Cannon-Bowers, J. A. (2002). What we know about designing and delivering team training: Tips and guidelines. In K. Kraiger (Ed.), *Creating, implementing, and managing effective training and development: State-of-the-art lessons for practice* (pp. 234–259). San Francisco, CA: Jossey-Bass.

Salas, E., & Cannon-Bowers, J. A. (2000). The anatomy of team training. In S. Tobias & J. D. Fletcher (Eds.), *Training and retraining* (pp. 312–338). New York, NY: Macmillan.

Salas, E., Klein, C., King, H., Salisbury, M., Augenstein, J. S., Birnbach, D. J., . . . Upshaw, C. (2008). Debriefing medical teams: 12 evidence-based best practices and tips. *The Joint Commission Journal on Quality and Patient Safety, 34*(9), 518–527.

Salas, E., Oser, R. L., Cannon-Bowers, J. A., & Daskarolis, E. (2002). Team training in virtual environments: An event-based approach. In K. M. Stanney (Ed.), *Handbook of virtual environments: Design, implementation and applications* (pp. 873–892). Mahwah, NJ: Lawrence Erlbaum Associates.

Salas, E., & Priest, H. A. (2005). Team training. In N. Stanton, A. Hedge, K. Brookhuis, E. Salas, & H. Hendrick (Eds.), *Handbook of human factors and ergonomics methods* (pp. 44-1–44-7). Boca Raton, FL: CRC Press.

Salas, E., Rosen, M. A., Weaver, S. J., Held, J. D., & Weissmuller, J. J. (2009). Guidelines for performance measurement in simulation-based training. *Ergonomics in Design, 17*(4), 12–18.

Salas, E., Tannenbaum, S. I., Kraiger, K., & Smith-Jentsch, K. A. (2012). The science of training and development in organizations: What matters in practice. *Psychological Science in the Public Interest, 13*(2), 74–101.

Salas, E., Weaver, S. J., DiazGranados, D., Lyons, R., & King, H. (2009). Sounding the call for team training in health care: Some insights and warnings. *Academic Medicine, 84*(10), 128–131.

Salas, E., Weaver, S. J., & Wildman, J. L. (2009). How to build expert teams: Best practices. In R. J. Burke & C. L. Cooper (Eds.), *The peak performing organization* (pp. 129–156). New York, NY: Routledge.

Salas, E., Wildman, J. L., & Piccolo, R. F. (2009). Using simulation-based training to enhance management education. *Academy of Management Learning and Education, 8*(4), 559–573.

Salas, E., Wilson, K. A., Burke, C. S., & Priest, H. A. (2006). What is simulation-based training? *Forum, 24*(2), 12.

Salas, E., Wilson, K. A., Priest, H. A., & Guthrie, J. W. (2006). Design, delivery, and evaluation of training systems. In G. Salvendy (Ed.), *Handbook of human factors and ergonomics* (3rd ed., pp. 472–512). Hoboken, NJ: John Wiley & Sons.

Salas, E., Wilson-Donnelly, K. A., Sims, D. E., Burke, C. S., & Priest, H. A. (2007). Teamwork training for patient safety: Best practices and guiding principles. In C. Pascale (Ed.), *Handbook of human factors and ergonomics in health care and patient safety* (pp. 803–822). Mahwah, NJ: Lawrence Erlbaum Associates.

Shuffler, M. L., Salas, E., & Xavier, L. F. (2010). The design, delivery, and evaluation of crew resource management. In B. Kanki, R. Helmreich, & J. Anca (Eds.), *Crew resource management* (pp. 205–232). San Diego, CA: Elsevier.

Smith-Jentsch, K. A., Baker, D. P., Salas, E., & Cannon-Bowers, J. A. (2001). Uncovering differences in team competency requirements: The case of air traffic control teams. In E. Salas, C. A. Bowers, & E. Edens (Eds.), *Improving teamwork in organizations: Applications of resource management training* (pp. 31–54). Mahwah, NJ: Lawrence Erlbaum Associates.

Smith-Jentsch, K. A., Cannon-Bowers, J. A., Tannenbaum, S. I., & Salas, E. (2008). Guided team self-correction: Impacts on team mental models, processes, and effectiveness. *Journal of Small Group Research, 39*(3), 303–327.

Stevens, M. J., & Campion, M. A. (1994). The knowledge, skill, and ability requirements for teamwork: Implications for human resource management. *Journal of Management, 20*(2), 503–530.

Tannenbaum, S. I., & Cerasoli, C. P. (2013). Do team and individual debriefs enhance performance? A meta-analysis. *Human Factors: The Journal of the Human Factors and Ergonomics Society, 55*(1), 231–245.

Tannenbaum, S. I., Smith-Jentsch, K. A., & Behson, S. J. (1998). Training team leaders to facilitate team learning and performance. In J. A. Cannon-Bowers & E. Salas (Eds.), *Decision making under stress: Implications for training and simulation* (pp. 247–270). Washington, DC: APA Press.

Weaver, S. J., Salas, E., & King, H. B. (2011). Twelve best practices for team training evaluation in health care. *The Joint Commission Journal on Quality and Patient Safety, 37*(8), 341–349.

Weaver, S.J., Salas, E., King, H., & DiazGranados, D. (2008). Does team training work? Principles for health care. *Society for Academic Emergency Medicine, 15*(11), 1002–1009.

Weaver, S. J., Salas, E., & Rosen, M. A. (2009). Managing team performance in complex settings: Research-based best practices. In J. W. Smither & M. London (Eds.), *Performance management: Putting research into action* (pp. 197–232). San Francisco, CA: Jossey-Bass.

Wildman, J. L., Salas, E., Priest, H. A., Lyons, R., & Carnegie, D. (2009). Managing virtual teams: Strategies for team leaders. *Ergonomics in Design, 17*(1), 8–13.

Wilson, K. A., Salas, E., & Lyons, R. (2008). Designing and delivering training for multicultural interactions in organizations. In D. Stone & E. Stone-Romero (Eds.), *The Influence of culture on human resource management processes and practices* (pp.115–134). New York, NY: Taylor & Francis Group.

Wilson-Donnelly, K., Priest, H., Salas, E., & Burke, C. (2005). The impact of organizational practices on safety in manufacturing: A review and reappraisal. *Human factors and ergonomics in manufacturing, 15*(2), 135–176.

# 7

# CONCLUDING REMARKS

The purpose of this book was to collate the wealth of knowledge on training, teams, and team training into a form that was insightful and comprehensive, yet simultaneously practical and helpful. To accomplish this, we incorporated a wealth of existing research and the practical experiences and knowledge of many experts in the fields of training and teams. This review and synthesis process went through much iteration, as the authors discussed (and at times debated) the best way to present the massive amount of information in ways that were engaging, comprehensive, and practical. One key consideration was how best to "slice" the team training literature. For example, Salas, Tannenbaum, Kraiger, and Smith-Jentsch (2012) divided important aspects of training into before, during, and after components and offered a checklist of steps to take during each phase (see Appendix 5). While we agree with the value of this advice and encourage those interested in team training to follow it, we felt there was too much overlap in the fundamental components of team training to present these concepts in a purely temporal fashion.

Ultimately, we arrived at five "pillars" of team training—the foundational components to consider when designing, implementing, delivering, evaluating, and sustaining team training. Briefly, these pillars encourage the training developer to: (1) Ensure the need for training, (2) Establish a climate that supports learning within the training setting, (3) Design and develop the training such that it maximizes accessibility, usability, and engagement, (4) Evaluate the effectiveness of team training, and (5) Help establish a system that will ensure the long-term effectiveness of team training. It is unnecessary here to reiterate or reword specific points made throughout the bulk of this book. Rather, in this concluding remarks chapter, we offer the reader some summative thoughts and concepts that span the five pillars but may or may not have been explicitly stated to this point.

## The Science of Team Training

As should be abundantly clear from the plethora of tips, advice, and guidelines we present in this book—and the references that accompany each of these—there is definitely a well-established science behind teamwork and training. For the past few decades, researchers have been exploring what drives effective team performance, what makes for an effective learning and training program, and how to best design and deliver effective team training programs. From this wealth of research, it is possible to develop science-driven developmental interventions. This is not simply a marketing ploy intended to impress organizational clients—an intervention being "science-driven" means that it is established upon the same principles and techniques that have yielded effective developmental outcomes in a wide array of settings and contexts. Unfortunately, having a wealth of knowledge at our disposal is meaningless unless it is actually applied to real team training interventions, and this is much easier said than done. Indeed, team developmental interventions can range from somewhat unproven team-building exercises (e.g., weekend retreats, ropes courses, trust falls) to homegrown interventions that are certainly ineffective and potentially dangerous. To illustrate the latter, consider the "waterboarding company" in which a particular sales manager attempted to motivate his team by staging a mock waterboarding (Vick, 2008). This exercise—which had no basis in scientific evidence or best practice whatsoever—was nevertheless conducted with the positive intent of motivating and building teamwork, and it points to the need to develop and deliver training systematically and with the backing of scientific evidence. On a less extreme note, a recent survey by the American Society for Training and Development (Paradise & Patel, 2009) suggested that barely one-fourth of organizations feel as if they get meaningful return on investment for all the time, effort, and money that is dumped in to training and developmental interventions. Systematic team training interventions grounded in solid scientific evidence promise to substantially increase this number.

To offer one final illustration on the importance of science to the field of training and team development, consider again the medical doctor analogy presented in Chapter 2. Earlier, we suggested that team training interventions are like a medicine that is administered to address a specific illness—if the medical diagnostic process (i.e., team training needs analysis) determines that there is an illness (i.e., organizational problem) that could be solved by a particular intervention, medicine, or procedure, that intervention (i.e., team training) is prescribed. Expanding this analogy, consider the team trainer (or team of trainers including designers, developers, facilitators, and evaluators) as a doctor or medical team. One would hope that this medical team is basing their practice, including diagnostic processes, selecting medicines, and performing different medical procedures, on sound medical science rather than conjecture or anecdotal evidence. Similarly, organizational interventions should aspire to high levels of precision and effectiveness—goals that can only be attained when relying on sound scientific evidence.

## What Team Training Is NOT

Beyond simply reminding trainers and organizations to use the science of team training (Hollenbeck, DeRue, & Guzzo, 2004; Shuffler, DiazGranados, & Salas, 2011; Tannenbaum & Yukl, 1992)—a task we have hopefully made simpler through the development of this book—we offer the reader four things that team training is NOT. While we define team training clearly in Chapter 1, it is appropriate to bring this work full circle and provide further clarity by defining it in the negative. Briefly, four things that team training is not include: (1) a panacea, (2) a silver bullet, (3) a one-time intervention, and (4) a simple organizational intervention. These things that team training is not have been explicated time and again, and in different academic and practical contexts (e.g., Daniels, 2003; Salas, Wilson, Burke, & Priest, 2005; Tannenbaum & Yukl, 1992). Nonetheless, they also happen to be disastrous assumptions and missteps that trainers and organizations frequently make. In illustrating these four things, we bring greater awareness and understanding, with the hope that these will enable trainers and organizations to avoid these missteps.

### Team Training Is NOT a Panacea

As intimated in Pillar 1, team training is not a panacea. It is not a "cure for what ails" any and all organizational woes. In Pillar 1, we highlight the importance of the "team training needs analysis" (TTNA) for determining whether team training is appropriate and also for garnering support for team training from organizational leadership and other stakeholders. Again, it is unnecessary to simply restate the content of this first pillar of team training. However, given the call to establish a need for team training, it follows that there may be some organizational problems that will *not* be addressed by team training. Naturally, organizational problems that are unrelated or loosely related to teams—such as poor individual performance and ineffective leadership, or bad recruitment, selection, and retention practices—will not be solved by team training. These problems are better solved by more targeted solutions, for even the best team training intervention will not improve performance if the organization cannot attract (or keep) effective employees. Even between team training and team building, which are both classified as team development interventions, team building has advantages over team training in certain circumstances (though team training has more research behind it). Specifically, team building is thought to be better suited for improving team outcomes such as role clarity, trust, satisfaction, and conflict processes, whereas team training is more suited for cognitive processes and emergent states that are directly related to team performance (Shuffler et al., 2011). In other words, even when team processes have been identified as the root of poor organizational and team performance, there are some circumstances when team building may be more appropriate than team training.

Along with the notion of team training not being a panacea comes a warning to not be swayed by slick marketing or trendy practices—unless they are backed by solid evidence of effectiveness. The mark of a panacea or cure-all is that it claims to solve the world while offering little in the way of evidence. Team training programs that are high on promises but low on proof should be avoided. This is particularly salient when it comes to technology. High technology and realistic team simulations are exciting and may be quite easy to sell to organizational leadership simply based on the "cool factor." And indeed, the degree to which training content and delivery mechanisms are engaging are pieces of the team training puzzle. Yet simply engaging a group of learners does not constitute team training. The delivery must be engaging yes, but the content must be relevant, and it must engage the cognitive and group processes that drive performance in the workplace. Rather than getting hooked on an intervention that seems "too good to be true," it is essential to remember that team training is not a panacea—it will not solve every organizational problem, and higher-tech does not necessarily mean better.

## Team Training Is NOT a Silver Bullet

Assuming the team training needs analysis confirms that substandard performance is indeed due to team deficiencies in either teamwork or taskwork, and assuming that the content and delivery of the training is built on sound scientific evidence, does this mean that team training is guaranteed to be effective? Unfortunately, no. As with many things in organizational psychology (and business in general), there are mitigating conditions that prevent team training (even when it is appropriate) from being a "silver bullet"—a shot guaranteed to eliminate and counteract threats to organizational performance. Training developers, facilitators, and organizational leadership must be aware of these mitigating factors so that they might either circumvent them or address them head-on.

One of the things that most frequently prevents training from being effective even when it should be is the lack of supportive organizational conditions. We have discussed this at some length throughout the book thus far; nonetheless, there are a few key points that are worth highlighting as we conclude. First is the notion that "supportive" conditions exist on a continuum. Organizations may openly praise, reward, and encourage employees when they return from training and begin applying what they have learned on the job. At the other end of the spectrum, employees may actually be mocked by others, given more work, or otherwise punished for trying to apply training to the job—a phenomenon known as *sanctioning of transfer* (Holton, Bates, & Ruona, 2000). It is important here to mention that sanctioning of training transfer (and consequently, the supportiveness present within an organization) may come from multiple sources. Peers from other teams or departments may see individuals attempting to apply the learning from team training as fanatical, weird, or simply misaligned with the organizational culture. If these perceptions are communicated strongly enough, learners will feel unable to transfer training to the job. Similarly, supervisors may actively punish learners for attempting to apply training. While organizational support should have been assessed and/or established during the needs analysis, even a few unsupportive supervisors can derail learners' motivation for applying training to the job. In between the two extremes of support and sanctioning is indifference towards learning transfer, wherein employees are neither praised nor punished for transferring learning to the job, and organizational conditions remain largely unchanged.

The danger of indifference towards training transfer is not hard to see. In the landmark paper, "On the Folly of Rewarding 'A' While Hoping for 'B'," Kerr (1975) illustrated how organizations many times desire that one thing happens (e.g., transfer of training), but for whatever reason they reward a different thing (e.g., behaviors contrary to training emphases). The takeaway here is that *whatever gets rewarded gets repeated*. This is especially salient when it comes to training effectiveness in organizations, because it is not uncommon for organizational leadership to explicitly acknowledge the importance of a particular teamwork competency while, at the same time, implicitly engage in practices and implement policies that make applying trained teamwork competencies very difficult. For example, if an organization rewards sales teams strictly based on sales performance, teams with effective taskwork (i.e., sales) but ineffective teamwork will likely be unmotivated to risk changing their ways. The sentiment in this situation will be, "Why waste time and energy attempting to improve our teamwork if it's going to cost myself and the team performance numbers—and rewards?" Similarly, if organizational policies acknowledge and reward individual performance over team performance, it will be difficult for employees (and learners) to see good reasons for engaging in trained teamwork behaviors. Team training that *appears* effective in the training environment *will not and indeed cannot* overcome organizational conditions that are contrary to the consistent performance of trained teamwork competencies.

### Team Training Is NOT a One-Time Intervention

Supportive conditions are important for learners coming back from team training so that they are able and motivated to apply learning to the job immediately following training. However, supportive conditions and good long-term training systems are even more important for the long-term sustainability of team training effectiveness. Researchers estimate that somewhere between 50% (Saks, 2002) and 90% (Georgenson, 1982) of training content is not actually transferred to the workplace. Naturally, this number increases over time, as skills tend to decay as time progresses—and even more so in the absence of practice and supportive conditions. Indeed, a recent survey of training and development professionals suggested that up to 70% of training competencies are lost within a year of training (Saks, 2002). This should not be surprising, however. When training for physical fitness, it would be ridiculous to exercise once, or for one weekend, or for even an entire week, and then say, "I am done. I am physically fit." Similarly, teamwork competencies are "muscles" that need to be trained and consistently exercised.

This means that team training is not a one-and-done proposition. It requires repeated monitoring and refreshing. Evaluation over time is essential—as we suggest in Pillar 4—to allow the organization to identify important indicators and predictors of training effectiveness. For example, continuous evaluation should prevent trained competencies from decaying to unacceptable levels. That is, if evaluation processes identify that trained skills have decayed, it would be recommended to provide refresher training. It might also focus on changes in the presence of barriers to training transfer, such as might occur when a new leader joins the organization but does not actively support trained team competencies. Beyond frequent monitoring (and refresher training when necessary), team training should not be expected to be effective in isolation—other supplementary interventions may be necessary (e.g., rewarding teamwork behaviors, providing job aids/reminders to facilitate transfer). Ultimately, monitoring and providing resources should be seen not as a burden or obligatory element of team training, but as an asset for management and protection. Training is expensive—indeed, the Association for Talent Development (formerly the American Society for Training and Development) estimates that in 2011, organizations spent over $156 billion on employee training and development, or approximately $1,200 per year per person. Despite these massive expenses, skill decay through nonuse or barriers to training transfer can rob organizations of that investment.

## Team Training Is NOT a Simple Organizational Intervention

If one thing should be clear by now from the information presented within this book, it is that team training is *complex*. Team training requires careful assessment and evaluation, delivery targeted to specific teamwork competencies, and the support of a variety of stakeholders, prior to, during, and after team training. Team training is not about coming up with something that "seems reasonable." Indeed, this mentality was likely at least partly to blame behind the "waterboarding" team-building illustration provided earlier (Vick, 2008). This complexity means that team training itself requires teamwork. That is, no one person can effectively design, deliver, and evaluate team training. At the very least, when designing training, there must be a collaborative partnership between organizational subject matter experts (SMEs) and experts in learning and training design. Learning and training experts are essential to ensure that the training is developed and delivered in such a way that maximizes engagement, learning, and motivation and ability to transfer learned content. Organizational SMEs are needed to provide insights unique to the organization; that is, teamwork competencies that work at Retail Company "A" may be unnecessary at Manufacturing Corporation "B." Musson and Helmreich (2004) acknowledged this as well when warning the healthcare industry against uncritically adopting all of Crew Resource Management (CRM), a team training program designed within the context of the aviation industry. They argued that teamwork (and especially team-level taskwork) competencies relevant in the aviation industry may not be as relevant in the medical context.

Ultimately, organizational SMEs provide much of the content, while learning and training experts provide the process. When focusing on team training, experts in teamwork may be necessary too. Organizational SMEs may be aware of some generic teamwork competencies (and certainly specific task behaviors) that are important for performance, but they may not be aware of the complexity of teamwork competencies and behaviors that drive team performance. Therefore, a partnership between organizational SMEs and teamwork experts is especially important as well. An added benefit of this partnership with organizational SMEs is garnering support from stakeholders within the organization. When key members of an organization participate in the development of training, they feel more invested and engaged in it, which may lead them to support it more vocally. Furthermore, by ensuring that the content is relevant to the specifics of the organization, the training is and appears more valid—this perception is earning the interest and support of stakeholders and potential learners.

Teams, training, and team training are huge fields of practical application and ongoing research, and this will continue to grow as organizations increasingly look to team-based structures to gain a competitive advantage. Teamwork, especially in complex environments, is generally unnatural (though there are extremely rare cases when it may come naturally), and can therefore be quite difficult to manage, lead, or train. It is the job of the training professional to design, develop, deliver, and evaluate training programs that will help individuals, teams, and organizations improve the myriad knowledge, skills, and attitudes that serve as the foundation for effective team performance. To accomplish this lofty and complex goal, training professionals must rely on the plethora of scientific findings and validated best practices to *systematically* design and develop effective training programs. Furthermore, part of this systematic approach to the design and development of training should take into account the strong effects that organizational conditions can have on training outcomes. When solid research guides program development (but is flexible to organizational conditions), team training is more likely to be effective—and consistently so. While more research is always needed, there is a plethora of existing research currently available—as can be clearly seen from the development of this book. We hope that the ideas presented herein are comprehensive yet parsimonious, and practical in such a way that it will encourage training professionals to apply this knowledge that they now have at their disposal.

# References

Daniels, S. (2003). Employee training: A strategic approach to better return on investment. *Journal of Business Strategy, 24*, 39–42.

Georgenson, D.L. (1982). The problem of transfer calls for partnership. *Training and Development Journal, 36*(10), 75–78.

Hollenbeck, J.R., DeRue, D.S., & Guzzo, R. (2004). Bridging the gap between I/O research and HR practice: Improving team composition, team training, and team task design. *Human Resource Management, 43,* 353–366.

Holton, E.F., Bates, R.A. and Ruona, W.E.A. (2000). Development of a generalized learning transfer system inventory. *Human Resource Development Quarterly, 11*(4), 333–360.

Kerr, S. (1975). On the folly of rewarding A, while hoping for B. *Academy of Management Journal, 18*(4), 769–783.

Musson, D.M., & Helmreich, R.L. (2004). Team training and resource management in health care: Current issues and future directions. *Harvard Health Policy Review, 5,* 25–35.

Paradise, A., & Patel, L. (2009). *2009 state of the industry report: ASTD's annual review of trends in workplace learning and performance.* Alexandria, VA: ASTD.

Saks, A. M. (2002). So what is a good transfer of training estimate? A reply to Fitzpatrick. *The Industrial Organizational Psychologist, January 2002,* 29–30. Retrieved from www.siop.org/tip/backissues/TIPJan02/pdf/393_%20029to030.pdf

Salas, E., Tannenbaum, S. I., Kraiger, K., & Smith-Jentsch, K.A. (2012). The science of training and development in organizations: What matters in practice. *Psychological Science in the Public Interest, 13*(2), 74–101.

Salas, E., Wilson, K.A., Burke, C.S., & Priest, H.A. (2005). Using simulation-based training to improve patient safety: What does it take? *Journal on Quality and Patient Safety, 31,* 363–371.

Shuffler, M.L., DiazGranados, D., & Salas, E. (2011). There's a science for that: Team development interventions in organizations. *Current Directions in Psychological Science, 20*(6), 365–372.

Tannenbaum, S.I., & Yukl, G. (1992). Training and development in work organizations. *Annual Review of Psychology, 43,* 399–441.

Vick, K. (2008). Team-building or torture? Court will decide. *Washington Post.* Available from www.washingtonpost.com/wp-dyn/content/article/2008/04/12/AR2008041201739.html

# APPENDIX 1

Reprinted from Salas, E., Rosen, M. A., Burke, C. S., & Goodwin, G. F. (2009). The wisdom of collectives in organizations: An update of the teamwork competencies. In E. Salas, G. F. Goodwin, & C. S. Burke (Eds.), *Team effectiveness in complex organizations: Cross disciplinary perspectives and approaches* (pp. 39–79). New York, NY: Taylor & Francis Group.

[See pages 52–63.]

Note: + indicates substantial empirical support; ~ indicates moderate empirical support.

Summary of the ABCs of Teamwork (Attitudes)

| Proposed KSAs | Description | Example Behavioral Markers | Representative Sources | Empirical Evidence |
|---|---|---|---|---|
| Team/Collective Orientation | "A preference for working with others and the tendency to enhance individual performance through the coordination, evaluation, and utilization of task inputs from other group members while performing group tasks" (Salas, Guthrie, Wilson, Priest, & Burke, 2005, p. 200). | • Team members are accepting of input from other teammates; input is evaluated based on quality, not source.<br>• Team members have high levels of task involvement, information sharing, participatory goal setting, and strategizing.<br>• Team members value team goals over individual goals. | • Alavi & McCormick (2004)<br>• Driskell & Salas (1992)<br>• Eby & Dobbins (1997)<br>• Jackson, Colquitt, Wesson, & Zapata-Phelan (2006)<br>• Mohammed & Angell (2004)<br>• Salas, Sims, & Burke (2005) | + |
| Team/Collective Efficacy | "A sense of collective competence shared among individuals when allocating, coordinating, and integrating their resources in a successful concerted response to specific situational demands" (Zaccaro, Blair, Peterson, & Zazanis, 1995, p. 309). | • Team members have positive evaluations of their leader's ability.<br>• Team members share positive evaluations about the team's ability to accomplish its goals. | • Bandura (1986)<br>• Gibson (2003)<br>• Katz-Navon & Erez (2005)<br>• Watson, Chemers, & Preiser (2001)<br>• Zaccaro, Blair, Peterson, & Zazanis (1995) | + |
| Psychological Safety | "A shared belief that the team is safe for interpersonal risk taking" (Edmondson, 1999, p. 354). | • Team members believe other members have positive intentions.<br>• Team members aren't rejected for being themselves.<br>• Team members respect each other's abilities.<br>• Team members are interested in each other as people.<br>• Team members have high team efficacy. | • Edmondson (1999) | ? |

| Term | Definition | | References | |
|---|---|---|---|---|
| Team Learning Orientation | "A shared perception of team goals related to learning and competence development; goals that guide the extent, scope, and magnitude of learning behaviors pursued within a team" (Bunderson & Sutcliffe, 2003, p. 553). | • Team members seek and give feedback.<br>• Team members discuss errors.<br>• Team members experiment with processes and procedures.<br>• Team members make changes and improvements in processes.<br>• Team members seek information and feedback from outside the team.<br>• Team members manage conflict constructively. | • Bunderson & Sutcliffe (2003)<br>• Yazici (2005) | ~ |
| Team Cohesion | The degree to which team members exhibit interpersonal attraction, group pride, and commitment to the task. | • Team members have a shared task focus and commitment to attaining the goals of the team.<br>• Team members have a desire to remain a member of the team.<br>• Team members express pride associated with team membership. | • Beal, Cohen, Burke, & McLendon (2003)<br>• Carless & DePaola (2000)<br>• Zaccaro, Gualtieri, Minionis (1995) | + |
| Mutual Trust | "The shared belief that team members will perform their roles and protect the interests of their teammates" (Salas, Sims, & Burke, 2005, p. 561). | • Team members share a belief that team members will perform their tasks and roles.<br>• Team members share a belief that fellow team members will work to protect the interests of the team.<br>• Team members are willing to admit mistakes; they are not fearful of reprisal.<br>• Team members share information openly. | • Aubert & Kelsey (2003)<br>• Bandow (2001)<br>• Salas, Sims, & Burke (2005) | + |

*(Continued)*

Summary of the ABCs of Teamwork (Attitudes) (Continued)

| Proposed KSAs | Description | Example Behavioral Markers | Representative Sources | Empirical Evidence |
|---|---|---|---|---|
| Team Empowerment | "Team members' collective belief that they have the authority to control their proximal work environment and are responsible for their team's functioning" (Mathieu, Gilson, & Ruddy, 2006, p. 98). | • Team members decide which team processes to engage in and how to execute those processes. | • Mathieu, Gilson, & Ruddy (2006)<br>• Kirkman, Rosen, Tesluk, & Gibson (2004) | ? |
| Team Reward Attitude | "An individual's general evaluation of receiving rewards based on the performance of the team" (Shaw, Duffy, & Stark, 2001, p. 904). | • Team members have positive evaluations of rewarding team (versus individual) performance.<br>• Team members value teamwork. | • Haines & Taggar (2006)<br>• Shaw, Duffy, & Stark (2001) | ? |
| Team Goal Commitment/ Team Conscientiousness | The degree to which team members feel an attachment to the team level goal and the degree to which they are determined to reach this goal. | • Team members have common and valued goals.<br>• Team members monitor the team's progress toward its goals.<br>• Team members engage in supportive behaviors when necessary. | • Aubé & Rousseau (2005)<br>• English, Griffith, & Stellman (2004)<br>• Weldon & Weingart (1993) | ? |

Summary of the ABCs of Teamwork (Behaviors)

| Proposed KSAs | Description | Example Behavioral Markers | Representative Sources | Empirical Evidence |
|---|---|---|---|---|
| Mutual Performance Monitoring | The ability of team members to "keep track of fellow team members work while carrying out their own … to ensure that everything is running as expected" (McIntyre & Salas, 1995, p. 23). | • Team members recognize errors in their teammates' performance.<br>• Team members recognize superior performance in their teammates.<br>• Team members offer relevant information/ resources before requested.<br>• Team members have an accurate understanding of their teammates' workload.<br>• Team members offer feedback to their fellow teammates to facilitate self-correction. | • Dickinson & McIntyre (1997)<br>• Marks & Panzer (2004)<br>• Salas, Sims, & Burke (2005) | + |
| Adaptability | "Ability to adjust strategies based on information gathered from the environment through the use of backup behavior and reallocation of intrateam resources. Altering a course of action or team repertoire in response to changing conditions (internal or external)" (Salas, Sims, & Burke, p. 560). | • Team members modify or replace routine performance when characteristics of the environment and task change.<br>• Team members detect changes in the internal team and external environments.<br>• Team members make accurate assessments about underlying causes of environmental changes. | • Burke, Stagl, Salas, Pierce, & Kendall (2006)<br>• Entin & Serfaty (1999)<br>• Kozlowski, Gully, Nason, & Smith (1999)<br>• Salas, Sims, & Burke (2005) | + |

(Continued)

Summary of the ABCs of Teamwork (Behaviors) (Continued)

| Proposed KSAs | Description | Example Behavioral Markers | Representative Sources | Empirical Evidence |
|---|---|---|---|---|
| Backup/Supportive Behavior | "Ability to anticipate other team member's needs through accurate knowledge about their responsibilities. This includes the ability to shift workload among members to achieve balance during high periods of workload or pressure" (Salas, Sims, & Burke, 2005, p. 560). | • Team members proactively step in to assist fellow team members when need.<br>• Team members communicate the need for assistance.<br>• Team members can identify unbalanced workload distributions.<br>• Team members redistribute workload to underutilized team members. | • Marks, Mathieu, & Zaccaro (2001)<br>• McIntyre & Salas (1995)<br>• Porter et al. (2003)<br>• Salas, Sims, & Burke (2005) | + |
| Implicit Coordination Strategies | "Synchronization of members actions based on unspoken assumptions about what others in the group are likely to do" (Wittenbaum & Strasser, 1996, p. 23). | • Team members compensate for increasing workload conditions by reducing the "communication overhead" (i.e., explicit communication).<br>• Team members sequence interdependent taskwork without overt communication. | • Adelman, Miller, Henderson, & Schoelles (2003)<br>• Entin & Serfaty (1999)<br>• Espinosa, Lerch, & Kraut (2004)<br>• MacMillan, Entin, & Serfaty (2004)<br>• Rico, Sanchez-Manzanares, Gil, & Gibson (2008) | + |
| Shared/Distributed Leadership | "The transference of the leadership function among team members in order to take advantage of member strengths (e.g., knowledge, skills, attitudes, perspectives, contacts, and time available) as dicated by either environmental demands or the development stage of the team" (Burke, Fiore, & Salas, 2004, p. 105). | • Team members accurately recognize and identify the member with the highest levels of relevant knowledge and skill for a particular situation/problem.<br>• Team members shift leadership functions in response to changing task/ environmental conditions. | • Pearce & Sims (2002)<br>• Hiller, Day, & Vance (2006)<br>• Day, Gronn, & Salas (2004) | ? |

| Term | Definition | Behaviors | References | |
|---|---|---|---|---|
| Mission Analysis | "The interpretation and evaluation of the team's mission, including identification of its main tasks as well as the operative environmental conditions and team resources available for mission execution" (Marks, Mathieu, and Zaccaro, 2001, p. 365). | • Team members explicitly articulate the team's objectives.<br>• Team members discuss the purpose of the team in the context of the present performance environment.<br>• Team members discuss how the available team resources can be applied to meeting the team goals. | • Marks, Mathieu, & Zaccaro (2001)<br>• Mathieu & Schulze (2006) | ∼ |
| Problem Detection | An initial sensing that a problem requiring attention exists or will soon exist. | • Team members rapidly detect problems or potential problems in their environment.<br>• Team members work to determine underlying causes in conflicting knowledge.<br>• Team members quickly recognize a need for action when it arises.<br>• Team members clearly communicate problem definitions. | • Larson & Christensen (1993)<br>• Moreland & Levine (1992) | ∼ |
| Conflict Resolution/ Management | "Preemptive conflict management involves establishing conditions to prevent, control, or guide team conflict before it occurs. Reactive conflict management involves working through task and interpersonal disagreements among team members" (Marks, Mathieu, & Zaccaro, 2001, p. 361). | • Team members seek solutions that have mutual gains for all interests.<br>• Team members openly discuss task related conflict.<br>• Team members (find it acceptable to) change their minds and express their doubts. | • De Dreu & Weingart (2003)<br>• Gladstein (1984)<br>• Jehn (1995)<br>• Jordan & Troth (2004)<br>• Simons & Peterson (2000) | + |

(Continued)

Summary of the ABCs of Teamwork (Behaviors) (Continued)

| Proposed KSAs | Description | Example Behavioral Markers | Representative Sources | Empirical Evidence |
|---|---|---|---|---|
| Motivation of Others | Generating and maintaining goal directed effort toward completion of the team's mission. | • Team members encourage each other to perform better or to continue performing well.<br>• Team members provide feedback regarding team success.<br>• Team members communicate beliefs of the team's ability to succeed. | • Fleishman & Zaccaro (1992).<br>• Marks, Mathieu, & Zaccaro (2001) | ~ |
| Intrateam Feedback | The provision of information about team or individual performance either before, during, or after a performance episode. | • Team members engage in a cycle of prebrief, performance, debrief.<br>• Team members provide preperformance information (feed forward).<br>• Team members develop and integrate lessons learned from past performance.<br>• Team members provide information to correct deficient performance during a performance episode.<br>• Team members provide constructive and specific comments to other team members. | • Inzana, Driskell, Salas, & Johnston (1996)<br>• Smith–Jentsch, Johnston, & Payne (1998)<br>• Smith–Jentsch, Zeisig, Acton, & McPherson (1998) | + |
| Task-related Assertiveness | "The capacity to effectively communicate in interpersonal encounters by sharing ideas clearly and directly" (Pearsall & Ellis, 2006, p. 577). | • Team members communicate task-relevant information without hesitation.<br>• Team members share their opinions with others in a persuasive manner. | • Marks, Mathieu, & Zaccaro (2001)<br>• Pearsall & Ellis (2006)<br>• Smith–Jentsch, Salas, & Baker (1996) | + |

| | | | | |
|---|---|---|---|---|
| Planning | The generation of a proposed sequence of actions intended to accomplish a set goal. | • Team members explicitly articulate expectations for how a proposed course of action should unfold.<br>• Team members explicitly define desired outcomes.<br>• Team members collectively visualize how a planned course of action will be carried out and where it can go wrong.<br>• Team members seek out information and feed it to fellow team members.<br>• Team members share unique information. | • Klein & Miller (1999)<br>• Mathieu & Schulze (2006)<br>• Militello, Kyne, Klein, Getchell, & Thordsen (1999)<br>• Stout, Cannon-Bowers, Salas, & Milanovich (1999) | + |
| Coordination | "The process of orchestrating the sequence and timing of interdependent actions (Marks, Mathieu, & Zaccaro, 2001, pp. 367–368). | • Team taskwork behaviors are sequenced so that "down time" for team tasks is minimized (e.g., team members don't have to wait for other team members' input to do their taskwork).<br>• Team members communicate information about their status, needs, and objectives as often as necessary (and not more).<br>• Team members synchronize teamwork behaviors without overt communication in high-workload conditions.<br>• Team members pass information to one another relevant to the task in a timely and efficient manner. | • Brannick, Prince, Prince, & Salas (1995)<br>• Fleishman & Zaccaro (1992)<br>• Malone & Crowston (1994)<br>• Marks, Mathieu, & Zaccaro (2001)<br>• Smith-Jentsch, Johnston, & Payne (1998) | + |

(Continued)

Summary of the ABCs of Teamwork (Behaviors) (Continued)

| Proposed KSAs | Description | Example Behavioral Markers | Representative Sources | Empirical Evidence |
|---|---|---|---|---|
| Team Leadership | "Ability to direct and coordinate the activities of other team members, assess team performance, assign tasks, develop team knowledge, skills, and abilities, motivate team members, plan and organize, and establish a positive atmosphere" (Salas, Sims, & Burke, 2005, p. 560). | • Team leaders instill shared affects and motivation and define team goals with prebriefs.<br>• Team leaders promote team learning through two-way interactions in debriefs to generate lessons learned from performance episodes.<br>• Team leaders create team interdependencies.<br>• Team leaders communicate clear mission and vision for the team.<br>• Team leaders gather and provide performance relevant information to team members.<br>• Team leaders work to keep teams intact. | • Burke, Stagl, Salas, et al. (2006)<br>• Day, Gronn, & Salas (2004)<br>• Salas, Sims, & Burke (2005)<br>• Stagl, Salas, & Burke (2006)<br>• Zaccaro, Rittman, & Marks (2001) | + |
| Problem Solving | The process of (1) identifying and representing a discrepancy between the present and desired state of the environment and (2) discovering a means to close this "gap." | • Teams engage in contingency planning.<br>• Teams accurately recognize the internal expertise in the team and weights input accordingly.<br>• Team members accurately prioritize problem features.<br>• Team members dynamically assess and adjust their problem solution. | • Bonner (2004)<br>• Jordan & Troth (2004)<br>• Oser, Gualtieri, Cannon-Bowers, & Salas (1999) | + |

| Closed-loop Communication/ Information Exchange | A pattern of communication characterized by (1) a message being initiated by the sender, (2) the message being received, interpreted, and acknowledged by the intended receiver, and (3) a follow-up by the sender ensuring that the message was received and appropriately interpreted. | • Team members follow up to ensure that messages are received and understood.<br>• Team members acknowledge messages when they are sent.<br>• Team members cross check information with the sender to ensure that the message's meaning is understood.<br>• Team members provide "big picture" updates to one another as appropriate.<br>• Team members proactively pass information without being asked. | • Bowers, Jenstch, Salas, & Braun (1998)<br>• McIntyre & Salas (1995)<br>• Salas, Sims, & Burke (2005)<br>• Smith-Jentsch, Johnston, & Payne (1998)<br>• Smith-Jentsch, Zeisig, Acton, & McPherson (1998) | + |

Summary of the ABCs of Teamwork (Cognitions)

| Proposed KSAs | Description | Example Behavioral Markers | Representative Sources | Empirical Evidence |
|---|---|---|---|---|
| Rules for Matching a Situation with an Appropriate Action (Cue-Strategy Associations) | Team members have a repertoire of performance strategies and courses of action associated with frequently occurring situations and problems. | • Team members are able to rapidly recall an appropriate course of action when presented with a common situation and collectively decide on its fit with that situation.<br>• Team members shift strategies in response to changes in the task, team, and environment as appropriate. | • Cannon-Bowers & Salas (1997)<br>• Kline (2005)<br>• Stout, Cannon-Bowers, Salas, & Milanovich (1999) | + |
| Accurate Problem Models | "Shared understanding of the situation, the nature of the problem, the cause of the problem, the meaning of available cues, what is likely to happen in the future, with or without action by the team members, shared understanding of the goal or desired outcome, and a shared understanding of the solution strategy" (Orasanu, 1994, p. 259). | • Team members make compatible predictions about the consequences of proposed courses of action.<br>• Team members recognize the need for action and adjustments to planned courses of action when these solutions don't go as planned.<br>• Team members make similar judgments about the causes of successful and ineffectual plans.<br>• Team members engage in closed-loop communication to build this shared mental representation. | • Fiore & Schooler (2004)<br>• Orasanu (1990, 1994)<br>• Salas, Rosen, Burke, Nicholson, & Howse (2007) | + |

| Accurate and Shared Mental Models (Transactive Memory and Team Situational Awareness) | "An organized knowledge structure of the relationships among the task the team is engaged in and how the team members will interact" (Salas, Sims, & Burke, 2005, p. 561). | • Team members are able to recognize when other team members need information they have.<br>• Team members anticipate and predict the needs of their fellow team members.<br>• Team members implicitly adjust performance strategies to changing conditions in the team, task, and environment as needed.<br>• Team members use standardized terminology ("phraseology").<br>• Team members use concise communication.<br>• Team members have compatible explanations of task cues.<br>• Team members attempt to determine the underlying causes of conflicts in information.<br>• Team members actively seek information relevant to the task.<br>• Problems are explicitly defined.<br>• Team members engage in confirming and cross-checking information.<br>• Team members rapidly identify problems or potential problems. | • Artman (2000)<br>• Cannon-Bowers & Salas (1997)<br>• Cannon-Bowers, Tannenbaum, Salas, & Volpe (1995)<br>• Endsley (1995)<br>• Klein, Feltovich, Bradshaw, & Woods (2005)<br>• Klimoski & Mohammed (1994)<br>• Mathieu, Heffner, Goodwin, Salas, & Cannon-Bowers (2000)<br>• Salas, Cannon-Bowers, Fiore, & Stout (2001)<br>• Salas, Prince, Baker, & Shrestha (1995)<br>• Salas, Sims, & Burke (2005)<br>• Stout, Cannon-Bowers, & Salas (1996) | + |

(Continued)

Summary of the ABCs of Teamwork (Cognitions) (Continued)

| Proposed KSAs | Description | Example Behavioral Markers | Representative Sources | Empirical Evidence |
|---|---|---|---|---|
| Team Mission, Objectives, Norms, Resources | An understanding of the purpose, vision, and means available to the team for reaching the team objectives and completing the mission as well as the "shared expectations that constrain and drive the action of group members" (Graham, 2003, p. 323). | • Team members make compatible task prioritizations. Team members agree on the methods and approaches the team should take to work toward its goal (e.g., low task conflict related to selection of performance strategies). | • Cannon-Bowers & Salas (1997)<br>• Cannon-Bowers, Tannenbaum, Salas, & Volpe (1995)<br>• Marks, Mathieu, & Zaccaro (2001) | + |
| Understanding of Multiteam System (MTS) Couplings | An understanding in the team of how their performance (inputs, processes, and outcomes) is tied to the larger organizational structure, including other teams. | • Team members (especially leaders) understand the goal hierarchies in the larger organizational unit and work to meet these goals.<br>• Team members (especially leaders) engage in appropriate levels of effective conflict management with other team leaders in the MTS when different aspects of the goal hierarchy conflict. | • Hoegl, Weinkauf, & Gemueden (2004)<br>• Marks, DeChurch, Mathieu, Panzer, & Alonso (2005)<br>• Williams & Mahan (2006) | ? |

# References

Alavi, S.B., & McCormick, J. (2004). Theoretical and measurement issues for studies of collective orientation in team contexts. *Small Group Research, 35*(2), 111–127.

Artman, H. (2000). Team situation assessment and information distribution. *Ergonomics, 43*(8), 1111–1129.

Aubé, C., & Rousseau, V. (2005). Team goal commitment and team effectiveness: The role of task interdependence and supportive behaviors. *Group Dynamics: Theory, Research, and Practice, 9*(3), 189–204.

Aubert, B.A., & Kelsey, B.L. (2003). Further understanding of trust and performance in virtual teams. *Small Group Research, 34*(5), 575–618.

Bandow, D. (2001). Time to create sound teamwork. *Journal for Quality and Participation, 24*, 41–47.

Bandura, A. (1986). *Social foundations of thought and action: A social cognitive theory.* Englewood Cliffs, NY: Prentice-Hall.

Beal, D.J., Cohen, R.R., Burke, M.J., & McLendon, C.L. (2003). Cohesion and performance in groups: A meta-analytic clarification of construct relations. *Journal of Applied Psychology, 88*(6), 989–1004.

Bonner, B.L. (2004). Expertise in group problem solving: Recognition, social combination, and performance. *Group Dynamics: Theory, Research, and Practice, 8*(4), 277–290.

Bowers, C.A., Jentsch, F., Salas, E., & Braun, C.C. (1998). Analyzing communication sequences for team training needs assessment. *Human Factors, 40*(4), 672–679.

Brannick, M.T., Prince, A., Prince, C., & Salas, E. (1995). The measurement of team process. *Human Factors, 37*(3), 641–651.

Bunderson, J.S., & Sutcliffe, K.M. (2003). Management team learning orientation and business unit performance. *Journal of Applied Psychology, 88*(3), 552–560.

Burke, C.S., Stagl, K.C., Salas, E., Pierce, L., & Kendall, D. (2006). Understanding team adaptation: A conceptual analysis and model. *Journal of Applied Psychology, 91*, 1180–1207.

Cannon-Bowers, J.A., & Salas, E. (1997). Teamwork competencies: The interaction of team member knowledge, skills, and attitudes. In H.F. O'Neil, Jr. (Ed.), *Workforce readiness: Competencies and assessment* (pp. 151–174). Mahwah, NJ: Erlbaum.

Cannon-Bowers, J., Tannenbaum, S., Salas, E., & Volpe, C. (1995). Defining competencies and establishing team training requirements. *Team Effectiveness and Decision Making in Organizations, 1*, 333–380.

Carless, S.A., & DePaola, C. (2000). The measurement of cohesion in work teams. *Small Group Research, 37*(1), 71–88.

Day, D.V., Gronn, P., & Salas, E. (2004). Leadership capacity in teams. *Leadership Quarterly, 15*(6), 857–880.

De Dreu, C.K., & Weingart, L.R. (2003). Task versus relationship conflict, team performance, and team member satisfaction: A meta-analysis. *Journal of Applied Psychology, 88*(4), 741–749.

Dickinson, T.L., & McIntyre, R.M. (1997). A conceptual framework for teamwork measurement. In M.T. Brannick, E. Salas, & C. Prince (Eds.), *Team performance assessment and measurement: Theory, methods, and applications* (pp. 19–43). Mahwah, N.J.: Lawrence Erlbaum Associates.

Driskell, J.E., & Salas, E. (1992). Collective behavior and team performance. *Human Factors, 34*, 277–288.

Eby, L.T., & Dobbins, G.H. (1997). Collectivistic orientation in teams: An individual and group level analysis. *Journal of Organizational Behavior, 18*, 275–295.

Edmondson, A. (1999). Psychological safety and learning behavior in work teams. *Administrative Science Quarterly, 44*, 350–383.

Endsley, M.R. (1995). Toward a theory of situation awareness in dynamic systems. *Human Factors, 37*(1), 32–64.

English, A., Griffith, R.L., & Steelman, L.A. (2004). Team performance: The effect of team conscientiousness and task type. *Small Group Research, 35*(6), 643–665.

Entin, E.E., & Serfaty, D. (1999). Adaptive team coordination. *Human Factors, 41*(2), 312–325.

Espinosa, J.A., Lerch, F.J., & Kraut, R.E. (2004). Explicit versus implicit coordination mechanisms and task dependencies: One size does not fit all. In E. Salas & S.M. Fiore (Eds). *Team cognition: Understanding the factors that drive process and performance* (pp. 107–129). Washington, DC: American Psychological Association.

Fiore, S.M., & Schooler, W.J. (2004). Process mapping and shared cognition: Teamwork and the development of shared problem models. In E. Salas & S.M. Fiore (Eds.), *Team cognition: Understanding the factors that drive process and performance* (pp. 133–152). Washington, DC: American Psychological Association.

Fleishman, E.A., & Zaccaro, S.J. (1992). Toward a taxonomy of team performance functions. In R. Swezey & E. Salas (Eds.), *Teams: Their training and performance* (pp. 31–56). Norwood, NJ: Ablex.

Gibson, C.B. (2003). The efficacy advantage: Factors related to the formation of group efficacy. *Journal of Applied Social Psychology, 33*(10), 2153–2186.

Gladstein, D.L. (1984). Groups in context: A model of task group effectiveness. *Administrative Science Quarterly, 29*(4), 499–517.

Haines, V.Y., & Taggar, S. (2006). Antecedents of team reward attitude. *Journal of Management Review, 30*(2), 194–205.

Hiller, N.J., Day, D.V., & Vance, R.J. (2006). Collective enactment of leadership roles and team effectiveness: A field study. *The Leadership Quarterly, 17*, 387–397.

Hoegl, M., Weinkauf, K., & Gemueden, H.G. (2004). Interteam coordination, project committee, and teamwork in multiteam R&D projects: A longitudinal study. *Organizational Science, 15*(1), 38–55.

Inzana, C.M., Driskell, J.E., Salas, E., & Johnston, J.H. (1996). Effects of preparatory information on enhancing performance under stress. *Journal of Applied Psychology, 81*(4), 429–435.

Jackson, C.L., Colquitt, J.A., Wesson, M.J., & Zapata-Phelan, C.P. (2006). Psychological collectivism: A measurement validation and linkage to group member performance. *Journal of Applied Psychology, 91*(4), 884–899.

Jehn, K.A. (1995). A multimethod examination of the benefits and detriments of intragroup conflict. *Administrative Science Quarterly, 40*(2), 256–282.

Jordan, P.J., & Troth, A.C. (2004). Managing emotions during team problem solving: Emotional intelligence and conflict resolution. *Human Performance, 17*(2), 195–218.

Katz-Navon, T.Y., & Erez, M. (2005). When collective- and self-efficacy affect team performance: The role of task interdependence. *Small Group Research, 36*(4), 437–465.

Kirkman, B.L., Rosen, B., Tesluk, T., & Gibson, C. (2004). The impact of team empowerment on virtual team performance: The moderating role of face-to-face interaction. *Academy of Management Journal, 47*, 175–192.

Klein, G., Feltovich, P.J., Bradshaw, J.M., & Woods, D.D. (2005). Common ground and coordination in joint activity. In W.B. Rouse & K.R. Boff (Eds.), *Organizational Simulation* (pp. 139–184). Hoboken, NJ: Wiley-Interscience.

Klein, G., & Miller, T.F. (1999). Distributed planning teams. *International Journal of Cognitive Ergonomics, 3*(3), 203–222.

Klimoski, R., & Mohammed, S. (1994). Team mental model: Construct or metaphor? *Journal of Management, 20*(2), 403–437.

Kline, D.A. (2005). Intuitive team decision making. In H. Montgomery, R. Lipschitz, & B. Brehmer (Eds.), *How professionals make decisions* (pp. 171–182). Mahwah, NJ: Erlbaum.

Kozlowski, S.W.J., Gully, S.M., Nason, E.R., & Smith, E.M. (1999). Developing adaptive teams: A theory of compilation and performance across levels and time. In Dr. Ilgen & E.D. Pulakos (Eds.), *The changing nature of work and performance: Implications for staffing, personnel actions, and development.* San Francisco: Jossey-Bass.

Larson, J.R., & Christensen, C. (1993). Groups as problem-solving units: Toward a new meaning of social cognition. *British Journal of Social Psychology, 32,* 5–30.

MacMillan, J., Entin, E.E., & Serfaty, D. (2004). Communication overhead: The hidden cost of team cognition. In E. Salas & S.M. Fiore (Eds.), *Team cognition: Understanding the factors that drive process and performance* (pp. 61–82). Washington, DC: American Psychological Association.

Malone, T.W., & Crowston, K. (1994). The interdisciplinary study of coordination. *ACM Computing Surveys, 26*(1), 87–119.

Marks, M.A., DeChurch, L.A., Mathieu, J.E., Panzer, F.J., & Alonso, A. (2005). Teamwork in multiteam systems. *Journal of Applied Psychology, 90*(5), 964–971.

Marks, M.A., Mathieu, J.E., & Zaccaro, J. (2001). A temporally based framework and taxonomy of team processes. *The Academy of Management Review, 26*(3), 356–376.

Marks, M.A., & Panzer, F.J. (2004). The influence of team monitoring on team processes and performance. *Human Performance, 17*(1), 25–41.

Mathieu, J.E., Gilson, L.L., & Ruddy, T.M. (2006). Empowerment and team effectiveness: An empirical test of an integrated model. *Journal of Applied Psychology, 91*(1), 97–108.

Mathieu, J.E., & Schulze, W. (2006). The influence of team knowledge and formal plans on episodic team process-performance relationships. *Academy of Management Journal, 49*(3), 605–619.

McIntyre, R.M., & Salas, E. (1995). Measuring and managing for team performance: Emerging principles from complex environments. In R.A. Guzzo & E. Salas (Eds.), *Team effectiveness and decision making in organizations* (pp. 9–45). San Francisco: Jossey-Bass.

Militello, L.G., Kyne, M.M., Klein, G., Getchell, K., & Thordsen, M. (1999). A synthesized model of team performance. *International Journal of Cognitive Ergonomics, 3*(2), 131–158.

Mohammed, S., & Angell, L.C. (2004). Surface- and deep-level diversity in workgroups: Examining the moderating effects of team orientation and team process on relationship conflict. *Journal of Organizational Behavior, 25*(8), 1015–1039.

Moreland, R.L., & Levine, J.M. (1992). The composition of small groups. In E.J. Lawler, B. Markovsky, & H.A. Walker (Eds.), *Advances in Group Processes* (pp. 237–280). Greenwich, CT: JAI Press.

Orasanu, J. (1990). *Shared mental models and crew decision making* (No. 46). Princeton, NJ: Princeton University, Cognitive Science Laboratory.

Orasanu, J. (1994). Shared problem models and flight crew performance. In N. Johnston, N. McDonald, & R. Fuller (Eds.), *Aviation psychology in practice* (pp. 255–285). Brookfield, VT: Ashgate.

Oser, R.L., Gualtieri, J.W., Cannon-Bowers, J.A., & Salas, E. (1999). Training team problem solving skills: An event-based approach. *Computers in Human Behavior, 15,* 441–462.

Pearce, C.L., & Sims, H.P. (2002). Vertical versus shared leadership as predictors of the effectiveness of change management teams: An examination of aversive, directive, transactional, transformational, and empowering leader behaviors. *Group Dynamics: Theory, Research, and Practice, 6*(2), 172–197.

Pearsall, M.J., & Ellis, A.P.J. (2006). The effects of critical team member assertiveness on team performance and satisfaction. *Journal of Management, 32*(4), 575–594.

Porter, C.O., Hollenbeck, J.R., Ilgen, D.R., Ellis, A.P., West, B.J., & Moon, H. (2003). Backing up behaviors in teams: The role of personality and legitimacy of need. *Journal of Applied Psychology, 88*(3), 391–403.

Rico, R., Sanchez-Manzanares, M., Gil, F., & Gibson, C. (2008). Team implicit coordination processes: A team knowledge-based approach. *The Academy of Management Review, 33*(1), 163–184.

Salas, E., Cannon-Bowers, J.A., Fiore, S.M., & Stout, R.J. (2001). Cue-recognition training to enhance team situation awareness. In M. McNeese, E. Salas, & M. Endsley (Eds.), *New trends in collaborative activities: Understanding system dynamics in complex environments* (pp. 169–190). Santa Monica, CA: Human Factors and Ergonomics Society.

Salas, E., Guthrie Jr., J.W., Wilson, K.A., Priest, H.A., & Burke, C.S. Modeling team performance: The basic ingredients and research needs. In W.B. Rouse & K.R. Boff (Eds.), *Organizational simulation* (pp. 185–228). Hoboken, NJ: John Wiley & Sons.

Salas, E., Prince, C., Baker, D.P., & Shrestha, L. (1995). Situation awareness in team performance: Implications for measurement and training. *Human Factors, 37*(1), 123–136.

Salas, E., Rosen, M.A., Burke, C.S., Nicholson, D., & Howse, W.R. (2007). Markers for enhancing team cognition in complex environments: The power of team performance diagnosis. *Aviation, Space, and Environmental Medicine, 78*(5), B77–B85.

Salas, E., Sims, D.E., & Burke, C.S. (2005). Is there a big five in teamwork? *Small Group Research, 36*(5), 555–599.

Shaw, J.D., Duffy, M.K., & Stark, E.M. (2001). Team reward attitude: Construct development and initial validation. *Journal of Organizational Behavior, 22*, 903–917.

Simons, T.L., & Peterson, R.S. (2000). Task conflict and relationship conflict in top management teams: The pivotal role of intragroup trust. *Journal of Applied Psychology, 85*(1), 102–111.

Smith-Jentsch, K.A., Johnston, J.A., & Payne, S.C. (1998). Measuring team-related expertise in complex environments. In J.A. Cannon-Bowers & E. Salas (Eds.), *Making decisions under stress: Implications for individual and team training* (pp. 61–87). Washington DC: American Psychological Association.

Smith-Jentsch, K.A., Salas, E., & Baker, D.P. (1996). Training team performance-related assertiveness. *Personnel Psychology, 49*(4), 909–936.

Smith-Jentsch, K.A., Zeisig, R.L., Acton, B., & McPherson, J.A. (1998). Team dimensional training: A strategy for guided team self-correction. In J.A. Cannon-Bowers & E. Salas (Eds.), *Making decisions under stress: Implications for individual and team training* (pp. 271–297). Washington, DC: American Psychological Association.

Stagl, K.C., Salas, E., & Burke, C.S. (2006). Best practices in team leadership: What team leaders do to facilitate team effectiveness. In J.A. Conger & R.E. Riggio (Eds.), *The practice of leadership: Developing the next generation of leaders* (pp. 172–198). Hoboken, NJ: John Wiley & Sons.

Stout, R.J., Cannon-Bowers, J.A., & Salas, E. (1996). The role of shared mental models in developing situational awareness: Implications for training. *Training Research Journal, 2*, 85–116.

Stout, R.J., Cannon-Bowers, J.A., Salas, E., & Milanovich, D.M. (1999). Planning, shared mental models, and coordinated performance: An empirical link is established. *Human Factors, 41*(1), 61–71.

Watson, C.B., Chemers, M.M., & Preiser, N. (2001). Collective efficacy: A multilevel analysis. *Personality and Social Psychology Bulletin, 27*(8), 1057–1068.

Weldon, E., & Weingart, L.R. (1993). Group goals and group performance. *British Journal of Social Psychology, 32*(4), 307–328.

Williams, C.C., & Mahan, R.P. (2006). Understanding multiteam system functioning. In W. Bennett, Jr., C.E. Lance, & D.J. Woehr (Eds.), *Performance measurement: Current perspectives and future challenges* (pp. 205–224). Mahwah, NJ: Erlbaum.

Yazici, H.J. (2005). A study of collaborative learning style and team learning performance. *Education and Training, 47*(3), 216–229.

Zaccaro, S.J., Blair, V., Peterson, C., & Zazanis, M. (1995). Collective efficacy. In J.E. Maddux (Ed.), *Self-efficacy, adaptation, and adjustment: Theory, research, and application.* New York, NY: Plenum.

Zaccaro, S.J., Gualtieri, J., & Minionis, D. (1995). Task cohesion as a facilitator of team decision making under temporal urgency. *Military Psychology, 7*(2), 77–93.

Zaccaro, S.J., Rittman, A.L., & Marks, M.A. (2001). Team leadership. *Leadership Quarterly, 12*, 451–483.

# APPENDIX 2

## Example Subject Matter Expert Interview Protocol

### Introductions

Start by explaining who you are, who you might be working with (e.g., a university partner, government partner, commercial partner) and what the goal of the interview will be. For instance, you might let the subject matter expert (SME) know that you are working to develop training that will help the SME's team work together more cohesively and better coordinate efforts among the team to improve performance, manage conflict, or adapt to rapidly changing task conditions by improving communication, coordination, and cooperation.

You might also want to record information so that key data are not missed. Transcribed notes can be studied to find thematic themes across SMEs. If you decide to record the interview, be sure to ask the SMEs for their permission before or after the interview, reminding them that everything they say will be strictly confidential and that their participation in the interview is completely voluntary. Use of digital recordings might require additional consideration and justification by your organization's institutional review board. Be sure to check your organization's policy for conducting human subject research prior to starting interviews.

> To ensure SME responses are confidential and anonymous, assign participants a randomly generated numerical ID (e.g., 4 digits). Do not link names to this number. Also make sure to talk about other team members in terms of role, not by their name.

You should also point out that you plan to take notes during the interview—again reinforcing that all content will be confidential. You may also need to give the SME a heads up that you might need to ask for clarification at certain points during the interview (e.g., if acronyms are used) to make sure you are on the same page. Your introduction should also provide a clear picture of why you felt the interviewee would be a valuable SME. To conclude the introductions, explain the overall interview process. For example:

- We will be asking you about your thoughts and experiences, and gaining your perspective on a few key areas: communication, coordination, leadership, stress, and team performance.
- The interview will last approximately 60 minutes.
- Your participation is strictly voluntary and you are in no way required to provide information if you choose not to at any point. Our entire conversation today will be kept strictly confidential and no identifying information (i.e., your name) will be associated with your responses.
- Do you have any questions before we begin?

When the interview is complete, be sure to thank the SME for his/her time. Also provide him/her with contact information if in case he/she has any questions or anything else he/she might want to convey.

## Example Questions

These questions are presented as a guide for conducting SME interviews. Depending on the length or focus of the interview, you may decide to be more generic or explicit with the questions you ask. Additionally, it is beyond the scope of this book to provide examples for every type of team, task, and organization. Therefore, these examples focus primarily on overarching team concepts. Be sure to tailor questions to your unique purposes. For instance, you may be interested in how work conditions can be stressful and how stress may influence team functioning. SME interviews should be tailored accordingly.

### *Background Questions*

To start, we'd like to ask you a few questions about your background in general.

- What is your current role at this organization [insert organization name]?
- How long have you been with this organization [insert organization name]?
- How long have you been in your current role?

### *Questions about Team Composition and Processes*

*General Questions about Team Composition and Team Effectiveness:*

- Thinking back to your prior experiences within this department, if you were to describe who was on your team, who would you say?

- o   Do you consider members of other departments/units to be a part of your team?
    - ▪   Why or why not?
- o   Is there staff in this department that you don't consider as part of your team?
    - ▪   Why or why not?
- Thinking back on your experience, how would you describe the most effective team you have worked with?
    - o   What was it that made this team so effective?
    - o   What do you think are the three most important characteristics that a team member must have in order to be successful at:
        - ▪   Completing his/her own tasks?
        - ▪   Working as part of the team (e.g., coordinating and cooperating with other team members)?
        - ▪   Leading other team members?
        - ▪   Dealing with stress/workload?
- How would you describe the least effective team you have worked with
    - o   What was it that made this team so ineffective?
    - o   If there was one thing you could change that would improve the performance of this team, what would it be and why?


## Coordination:

### Within Team Coordination Requirements

- Thinking back on your prior experiences within [this team], to what degree do you think the tasks that you completed required the exchange of information or coordination of efforts among team members?
    - o   What are the top three factors that facilitate effective information exchange/coordination?
    - o   What are the top three barriers/disruptors of effective information exchange/coordination?
    - o   What tasks require more intensive coordination among team members?
    - o   What percentage of the tasks/objectives associated with your work require coordination among the entire team and what percentage are completed primarily by individuals (or a subset of individuals within the team)?
        - ▪   About how much time do you typically spend a day on tasks that are shared among the entire team?
        - ▪   About how much time do you typically spend a day on tasks that are yours alone?


### Between Team Coordination Requirements

- Similarly, to what degree do you think the tasks that your team completes require the exchange of information or coordination of efforts with other teams within [this department, organization]?

o   What are the types of teams that you share the most interdependence with?
- What is the nature of the task/object that requires such a high degree of interdependence?

o   What are the types of teams that you share the least interdependence with?

## Communication:

- Can you tell me a little more about communication within [insert team]?
  o   What would you say are the top three mechanisms that facilitate effective communication within [insert team]?
  o   What would you say are the top three barriers/disruptors of effective communication within [insert team]?
  - Are there any particular challenges to effective communication between this team and other teams in the organization (or outside the organization)?
  o   If you could suggest three things that would improve communication within [e.g., your team, your department, your organization], what would they be and why?

## Cooperation:

- Based on your experience, what is the level of cooperation required by members of your team?
  o   What are the top three mechanisms that facilitate effective cooperation?
  o   What are the three most significant barriers/disruptors of effective cooperation?
  o   If you could suggest three things that would improve the level of cooperation within [e.g., your team, your department, your organization], what would they be and why?
- Do you ever work on or help a colleague with tasks that were not assigned to you originally, or that you are not responsible for?
  o   *If yes,* how common is this?

## Leadership, Chain of Command, and Decision Making

- Can you please describe the leadership structure within [e.g., your team, department]?
  o   How are leadership roles different among staff positions?
  - What is the role of _____ [insert type of leader, e.g., attending physician]?
  - What is the role of _____ [insert type of leader, e.g., the nurse manager]?

- How would you describe the best leader you have ever worked with during your time as a _____? What three things made this leader so effective?
- How would you describe the least effect leader you have ever worked with during your time as a _____? What three things made this leader so ineffective?
- Can you tell me a little bit about the chain of command and how decisions are made within your [e.g., your team, your department, your organization]?
  - o Can you describe the differences, if any, between decisions that influence you and your ability to finish your work and those that influence your entire team [or department]?
  - o Who participates in the decision-making process?
    - ▪ While we understand that a decision-making hierarchy may exist, are there circumstances where decision making is shared among team members?

## Questions about Organizational/Department Support

### Feedback

- How is your individual performance evaluated? How is your team's performance evaluated?
  - o What is considered good/poor individual performance and what is considered good/poor team performance?
- Do you get feedback with regards to your own individual performance? Similarly, does your team receive feedback about the entire team's performance?
  - o Is the feedback you receive formal or informal?
  - o How is feedback delivered (e.g., written/verbal)?
  - o When and how often do you receive feedback?
  - o Who provides feedback to you or your team?
  - o In what ways is the feedback you receive helpful in improving both your performance and your team's performance?
  - o If you could suggest three ways to improve the feedback process, what would they be and why?

### Training/Quality Improvement

- Does your organization provide any formal team training or has it been involved with quality improvement initiatives designed to improve teamwork?
  - o What specific training did you receive?
  - o Did you find training useful? How would you improve training?
  - o Do you think training will help negative outcomes (e.g., performance errors, safety-related harms)?

## *Section 8: General Wrap-Up Questions*

- What are the three most significant challenges to effective teamwork [e.g., in your team, your department, your organization]?
- What are the three most significant facilitators to effective teamwork [e.g., in your team, your department, your organization]?
- If you could suggest three ways that would improve team performance (or a specific team task or performance outcome such as quality of goods produced, safety of operations), what would they be and why?

# APPENDIX 3

Reprinted from Shuffler, M. L., DiazGranados, D., & Salas, E. (2011). There's a science for that: Team development interventions in organizations. *Current Directions in Psychological Science, 20*(6), 365–372.
[See page 369.]

Purposes and Targeted Knowledge, Skills, and Attitudes of Different Training Strategies

| Training Strategy | Purpose | Targeted Knowledge, Skills, and Attitudes (KSAs) | Sources |
|---|---|---|---|
| Cross-training | Teaches each team member the duties and responsibilities of his/her teammates | • Shared knowledge of tasks & responsibilities<br>• Mutual performance monitoring<br>• Back-up behaviors | Volpe, Cannon-Bowers, Salas, & Spector (1996) |
| Team self-correction training | Develops team's ability to diagnose teamwork breakdowns/issues within the team and reach effective solutions internally on a continual basis | • Mutual performance monitoring<br>• Effective communication<br>• Leadership | Smith-Jentsch, Cannon-Bowers, Tannenbaum, & Salas (2008) |
| Team-coordination training | Targets the improvements of a team's shared mental-model framework or facilitates a common understanding of issues related to achieving team goals | • Back-up behaviors<br>• Mutual performance monitoring<br>• Understanding of teamwork skills | Entin & Serfaty (1999) |
| Crew Resource Management (CRM) | Provides instructional strategies designed to improve teamwork by applying well-tested training tools (e.g., simulators, role playing) targeted at specific content | • Communication<br>• Briefing<br>• Back-up behaviors<br>• Decision making<br>• Team adaptability<br>• Shared situation awareness | Salas, Burke, Bowers, & Wilson (2001) |

# References

Entin, E., & Serfaty, D. (1999). Adaptive team coordination. *Human Factors, 41*, 312–325.

Salas, E., Burke, C.S., Bowers, C.A., & Wilson, K.A. (2001). Team training in the skies: Does crew resource management (CRM) training work? *Human Factors, 43*, 641–674.

Smith-Jentsch, K., Cannon-Bowers, J., Tannenbaum, S., & Salas, E. (2008). Guided team self-correction: Impacts on team mental models, processes, and effectiveness. *Small Group Research, 39*, 303–327.

Volpe, C., Cannon-Bowers, J., Salas, E., & Spector, P. (1996). The impact of cross-training on team functioning: An empirical investigation. *Human Factors, 38*, 87–100.

# APPENDIX 4

Reprinted from Gregory, M. E., Feitosa, J., Driskell, T., Salas, E., & Vessey, W.B. (2013). Designing, delivering, and evaluating training in organizations: Principles that work. In E. Salas, S. I. Tannenbaum, D. Cohen, G. Latham, (Eds.), *Developing and enhancing teamwork in organizations: Evidence-based best practices and guidelines* (pp. 441–487). San Francisco, CA: Jossey-Bass.
[See pages 463–464.]

Advantages and Limitations of Various Team Training Delivery Methods

| Method | Types | Effectiveness | Resources Required | Benefits | Drawbacks |
|---|---|---|---|---|---|
| Information | — | Should always be used | Some/More | Provides baseline knowledge and a mental model; ease of delivery; low cost; effective; ease of application | Best employed in conjunction with other methods |
| | Lectures | Effective | Some | Simple to create; not resource intensive | Can be ineffective if speaker is inexpressive |
| | Slide presentations | Effective | Some | Facilitates immediate learning | Can be perceived as uninteresting |
| | Handouts (workbooks, advanced organizers, packets) | Effective | More | Facilitates development of a shared mental model | Can be slightly resource intensive |
| Demonstration | — | More effective | More | Flexible; cost-effective | Best employed with information- and practice-based methods |
| | Multimedia (like video) | More effective | More | Can foster a shared mental model; easy to use if material already exists | Can be resource intensive if creation of multimedia is required |
| | In person (live skit, presentation of behavior) | More effective | More | Can foster a shared mental model; may be less resource intensive versus multimedia | Less consistency (versus multimedia) |
| Practice | — | Most effective | More/Most | Enhances transfer of training. Especially useful for infrequent and/or dangerous tasks | If not guided, can lead to unproductive or counterproductive outcomes |
| | Role play | Most effective | More | Cost-effective | Can be difficult to implement with a large number of trainees; requires training of "actors" |
| | High-fidelity simulation | Most effective | Most | Realistic | Expensive |

# APPENDIX 5

Reprinted from Salas, E., Tannenbaum, S. I., Kraiger, K., & Smith-Jentsch, K. A. (2012). The science of training in organizations: What matters in practice. *Psychological Science in the Public Interest, 13*(2), 74–101.
[See pages 85, 89, and 92.]

# Checklist of Considerations Before Training

| Step | Actions | Outcomes |
|------|---------|----------|
| ▫ Conduct training needs analysis | • Determine what needs to be trained, who needs to be trained, and what type of organizational system you are dealing with. | • Clarifies expected learning outcomes and provides guidance for training design and evaluation.<br>• Enhances training effectiveness. |
| ▫ Job-task analysis | • Specify work and competency requirements.<br>• Examine teamwork demands, if needed.<br>• Identify what trainees need to know vs. what trainees need to access.<br>• Consider conducting a cognitive task analysis for knowledge-based jobs. | • Ensures that the training provided will address real job requirements and demands. |
| ▫ Organizational analysis | • Examine strategic priorities and the culture, norms, resources, limitations, and support for training.<br>• Determine whether policies and procedures in place support training. | • Enables strategic resource-allocation decisions.<br>• Identifies how the work environment can support or hinder the training objectives. |
| ▫ Person analysis | • Uncover who needs training and determine what kind of training they need.<br>• Determine whether training must be adapted for some learners. | • Clarifies training demand and trainees' needs.<br>• Maximizes benefits of the training by ensuring fit with trainees' needs. |
| ▫ Prepare learning climate | | |
| ▫ Schedule training | • Schedule training close to when trainees will be able to use on the job what they have learned.<br>• Plan to offer refresher training when skill decay cannot be avoided. | • Reduces skill decay and atrophy. |
| ▫ Notify employees | • Communicate clear expectations about the training.<br>• Describe training as an "opportunity" without overselling.<br>• Inform employees about any post-training follow-up.<br>• Communicate the importance of training. | • Encourages the right attendees.<br>• Ensures trainees enter with appropriate expectations, which enhances readiness and learning. |
| ▫ Establish attendance policies | • Determine whether attendance should be mandatory.<br>• Use the mandatory label selectively. | • Helps ensure learner motivation and attendance. |

| Step | Actions | Outcomes |
|------|---------|----------|
| ▫ Prepare supervisors and learners | • Prepare supervisors to support their employees and send the right signals about training. | • Enhances employees' motivation to learn. |

## Checklist of Considerations During Training

| Step | Actions | Outcomes |
|------|---------|----------|
| ▫ Enable the right trainee mindset | | |
| ▫ Build self-efficacy | • Deliver training in a way that builds trainees' belief in their ability to learn and perform trained skills.<br>• Reinforce performance during training. | • Enhances motivation and increases perseverance when on the job. |
| ▫ Promote a learning orientation | • Encourage trainees to participate in training to learn rather than to appear capable. If most trainees will not have that orientation, design more structured training experiences. | • Leads to greater learning. |
| ▫ Boost motivation to learn | • Engage trainees and build their interest. Ensure that training is perceived as relevant and useful. Show why it benefits them. | • Leads to learning and positive reactions to learning; may encourage transfer back on the job. |
| ▫ Follow appropriate instructional principles | | |
| ▫ Use a valid training strategy and design | • Include these elements in training: provide information, give demonstrations of good/bad behaviors, allow trainees to practice, and give meaningful and diagnostic feedback. | • Helps trainees understand and practice the knowledge, skills, and abilities that they need to develop; allows for remediation. |
| ▫ Build in opportunities for trainees to engage in transfer-appropriate processing | • Incorporate features that require trainees to engage in the same cognitive processes during training that they will have in the transfer environment (e.g., sufficient variability and difficulty).<br>• Recognize that performance during training does not necessarily reflect trainees' ability to apply what they have learned in the transfer environment. | • Equips trainees to be better able to apply what they learned when performing their job. |

*(Continued)*

Checklist of Considerations During Training (Continued)

| Step | Actions | Outcomes |
|------|---------|----------|
| ▫ Promote self-regulation | • Maintain trainees' attention and keep them on task by encouraging self-monitoring. | • Allows trainees to monitor their progress toward goals; enhances learning. |
| ▫ Incorporate errors into the training | • Encourage trainees to make errors during training, but be sure to give guidance on managing and correcting the errors. | • Improves transfer of training and equips trainees to deal with challenges on the job. |
| ▫ Use technology-based training wisely | • Technology can be beneficial in training, but proceed with caution. Recognize that entertaining trainees is an insufficient return on investment. | • Optimizes individual learning. |
| ▫ Use computer-based training (CBT) correctly | • Ensure that any CBT is based on sound instructional design, for example, providing trainees with guidance and feedback.<br>• Recognize that not all training can be delivered via computer. | • Allows for self-paced learning. |
| ▫ Allow user control wisely | • Provide sufficient structure and guidance to trainees when allowing them to make decisions about their learning experience. | • Allows for individualized training experiences while ensuring trainees have appropriate learning experience. |
| ▫ Use simulation appropriately | • Best to train complex and dynamic skills, particularly those that may be dangerous.<br>• Ensure the simulation is job relevant, even if it is not identical to the job. The priority should be on psychological fidelity rather than physical fidelity.<br>• Build in opportunity for performance diagnosis and feedback. Guide the practice. | • Enhances learning and performance; allows trainees to practice dangerous tasks safely. |

Checklist of Considerations after Training

| Step | Actions | Outcomes |
|------|---------|----------|
| ▫ Ensure transfer of training<br>  ▫ Remove obstacles to transfer | • Ensure trainees have ample time and opportunities to use what they have learned. | • Increases transfer of training and reduces skill decay.<br>• Maintains employee motivation and self-efficacy. |

| Step | Actions | Outcomes |
|---|---|---|
| □ Provide tools and advice to supervisors | • Ensure supervisors are equipped to reinforce trained skills and can promote ongoing learning using on-the-job experiences. | • Enables employees to retain and extend what they learned in training. |
| □ Encourage use of real-world debriefs | • Reflect on and discuss trainees' on-the-job experiences that are related to training.<br>• Reinforce lessons learned, uncover challenges, and plan how to handle situations in the future. | • Promotes retention, self-efficacy, and motivation.<br>• Improves job performance; promotes adequate mental models. |
| □ Provide other reinforcement and support mechanisms | • Consider providing trainees with job aids or access to knowledge repositories or communities of practice to reinforce and support what they learned in training. | • Improves performance. |
| □ Evaluate team training | | |
| □ Clearly specify the purpose of evaluation | • Determine what you hope to accomplish by evaluating the training and link all subsequent decisions back to the purpose. | • Ensures that time spend evaluating training produces desired results. |
| □ Consider evaluating training at multiple levels | • Consider measuring reactions, learning, behavior, and results.<br>• Use precise affective, cognitive, and/or behavioral indicators to measure the intended learning outcomes as uncovered during the needs assessment. | • Allows well-grounded decisions about training, including any necessary modifications.<br>• Enables effective training to continue to be supported. |